COCKTAILS
and
MIXED DRINKS

To Joan
for nearly forty years my guide,
fellow-traveller and drinking
companion.

COCKTAILS *and* MIXED DRINKS

Anthony Hogg

HAMLYN

London · New York · Sydney · Toronto

ACKNOWLEDGEMENTS

Being more of a drinker than a dispenser, I am grateful
for the help and advice of two professional bartenders,
Mr Austin Day of the White Horse, Chilgrove, and
Mr Peter Brennan of the Mayfair Hotel, London, a past
president of the United Kingdom Bartenders' Guild.
The Guild's kind co-operation is acknowledged in my text.
  I would like to thank also my friend and neighbour,
Peter Stevens, formerly the proprietor of the Millstream
Hotel, Bosham, for his help and Messrs Michael Wadsley
and Keith Bean of the West Sussex Standards
Department for kindly checking my capacity tables.
  Acknowledgements with thanks are due to Lady
Herbert and the International Wine and Food Society
for their kind permission to quote respectively the verses
by Sir Alan Herbert and Martin Armstrong.

*The publishers would like to thank the following for their
help in sponsoring the colour photographs for this book:*
Liquore Galliano *(half-title page)*
Drambuie liqueur *(page 29)*
White Satin gin *(pages 30–31)*
Bacardi rum *(page 32)*
Remy Martin cognac *(page 57)*
Stolichnaya vodka *(page 58)*
Mumm champagne *(page 75)*
Olives from Spain *(page 93)*
Taunton Cider *(page 112)*

*Apollo glasses on page 19 kindly supplied by
The Ravenhead Company Limited.*
Photography by John Lee
Line drawings by Russell Coulson

Half-title page shows a Harvey Wallbanger

Published by
The Hamlyn Publishing Group Limited
London · New York · Sydney · Toronto
Astronaut House, Feltham, Middlesex, England
© Copyright The Hamlyn Publishing Group Limited 1979
Seventh impression 1983

ISBN 0 600 32028 6

Phototypeset by Tradespools Ltd, Frome, Somerset
Printed in Italy

CONTENTS

SETTING CUP SHOP

Fill up the bowl, then fill it high,
Fill up the glasses there ; for why
Should every creature drink but I ;
Why, man of morals, tell me why?

Abraham Cowley

This is a book for the amateur wishing to mix and serve drinks at home. I recommend anybody wanting to achieve professional standards to buy a copy of *International Guide to Drinks*, compiled by the United Kingdom Bartenders' Guild and published in paperback every few years. It is the profession's handbook for bartenders.

Formed in 1933, this professional association first held a European cocktail competition at Torquay in 1951 and there are now twenty-six 'guilds' around the world, forming the International Bartenders' Association (I.B.A.). Thanks to the I.B.A.'s international cocktail conventions, Pink Ladies have been shaken to perfection from Blackpool to Buenos Aires and many new recipes tried and accepted.

Bar Space Professional or amateur, a barman needs about 12 sq ft in which to work. A bar can be improvised with two tables, $2\frac{1}{2}$ ft high, one behind for the bottles, the other in front to provide a working surface, where – facing the customers – he prepares the drinks. The bar counter – heat-proof, stain-proof and easy to clean – can be 1 ft higher.

MEASURES AND GLASSES

I put these together because, with experience, glasses can become measures. In Britain the smallest practical unit of liquid capacity is the fluid ounce; in America it is a different fluid ounce or liquid ounce, and in Western Europe the centilitre.

Table I, comparing the three, shows that for practical bar purposes the difference between British and American ounces can be forgotten. The two systems differ because the Americans retained the gallon of Queen Anne's time (231 cubic inches) whereas the British changed, in 1824, to the Imperial gallon (277.42 cubic inches).

Though legislation controls the size of our 1-pint and $\frac{1}{2}$-pint tankards, wine glasses and tumblers can be of any capacity. There are, however, usual shapes and sizes, as illustrated on page 19.

The standard spirit bottle, completely full, holds $26\frac{2}{3}$ fl oz or 75 cl, though in practice, when corked, the average content is 72 cl. Most wine bottles hold 72 cl too, with small variations between regions. Within the E.E.C. (European Economic Community) standardisation is in progress; ultimately 10, 37.5, 50, 75 and 100 centilitres should become the principal bottles, these figures being their actual average contents.

Bar Measures The British fluid ounce equals 8 fluid drachms or drams. Thus a dram, one-eighth of a fluid ounce (a mere 3 centi-

Table I: Measures and glasses – equivalent capacities

(Table to two points of decimals)

Centilitres	U.K. fluid ounces	U.S.A. liquid or fluid ounces	
(cl)	(fl oz)	(lq oz)	*Remarks*
0.1	0.03	0.03	*Dash = 5 drops*
0.5	0.18	0.17	*Teaspoon = ⅛ fl oz*
			Dessertspoon = ¼ fl oz
1	0.35	0.34	*Tablespoon = ½ fl oz*
2	0.70	0.68	*6-out measure = ⅚ fl oz*
			5-out measure = 1 fl oz
3	1.06	1.01	*4-out measure = 1¼ fl oz*
4	1.40	1.35	*Pony (U.S.A.) = 1 fl oz (approx.)*
5	1.76	1.69	*Jigger (U.S.A.) = 1½ fl oz (approx.)*
6	2.11	2.03	
7	2.46	2.37	*Cocktail glasses vary from 2 to 3½ oz.*
8	2.82	2.71	*2½ oz is an average U.K. size*
9	3.17	3.04	
10	3.52	3.38	
11	3.87	3.72	
12	4.22	4.06	*4-oz wine glass (U.S.A.); a good size for*
13	4.58	4.40	*Sours, like vodka and tomato juice.*
14	4.93	4.73	*A U.K. size is a 5-oz wine glass.*
15	5.28	5.07	*14.2 cl = 5 fl oz = 1 Gill or Noggin*
16	5.63	5.41	
17	5.98	5.75	
18	6.34	6.09	
19	6.69	6.42	
20	7.04	6.77	
21	7.39	7.10	
22	7.74	7.44	
23	8.10	7.78	*23 cl = U.K. 8-oz wine glass*
24	8.45	8.12	
25	8.80	8.45	
26	9.15	8.80	
27	9.50	9.13	
28	9.85	9.47	*28.4 cl = 10 fl oz = U.K. half-pint.*
29	10.21	9.81	*Tumblers can be smaller, but 10 oz gives wider scope*
30	10.56	10.14	*33 cl = 12-oz wine glass*
50	17.60	16.91	*56 cl = U.K. pint*
75	26.40	25.36	*75 cl = One 'Reputed' Quart = usual wine bottle*
100	35.20	33.81	*100 cl = 1 litre*

1.14 litres = 40 fl oz = 8.0 gills = One Imperial Quart = ¼ Imperial Gallon.

Table II: Comparison of small measures

U.K.	U.S.A.

U.K.

1 Gill or Noggin = 14.2 cl
6 -out (of a Gill) = 2·37 cl
5 -out (of a Gill) = 2.84 cl
4 -out (of a Gill) = 3.55 cl
2 -out (of a Gill) = 7.10 cl

4 Gills = 1 Imperial Pint = 20 fl oz = 56.8 cl
2 pints = 1 Imperial Quart = 40 fl oz = 113.6 cl (U.K. large spirit bottle)
4 Quarts = 1 Imperial Gallon = 160 fl oz = 4.55 litres = 277.42 cubic inches

U.S.A.

Pony = 1 lq oz (approx.) = 2.96 cl
Jigger = $1\frac{1}{2}$ lq oz (approx.) = 4.44 cl
Pint = 16 lq oz = 47.32 cl
Quart = 32 lq oz = 94.64 cl
4 Quarts = 1 U.S. Gallon = 128 lq oz = 3.784 litres (0.833 Imperial Gallons) = 231 cubic inches

Table III: Conversion table

To change from	to	multiply by	To change from	to	multiply by
grams	ounces	0.035	centilitres	liquid ounces (U.S.A.)	0.338
ounces	grams	28.35	gallons (U.K.)	litres	4.50
kilograms	pounds	2.205	gallons (U.S.A.)	litres	3.80
pounds	kilograms	0.454	litres	centilitres	10.00
centilitres	fluid ounces (U.K.)	0.352			

Temperature
°F to °C deduct 32 and multiply by 5/9   °C to °F multiply by 9/5 and add 32

litres) is rather less than a teaspoonful. It makes one wonder if the expression 'a wee dram' originated as a practical joke. By law, bar measures in Britain for gin, rum, vodka and whisky, drunk on licensed premises, must be either 4-out, 5-out or 6-out, each of which means 'out of a gill'. The same measure must be used for all four, a notice stating the size in use being clearly displayed. Brandy and liqueurs are not controlled, neither are mixtures of three or more liquors.

Since a 75-cl bottle contains 72 cl of spirits, which is virtually five gills, a 4-out (4×5) gives 20 measures; a 5-out (5×5) 25 measures and a 6-out (6×5) 30 measures to a bottle. Many bars will also keep the large 2-out (2×5), 10 measures to a bottle, and some use a 3-out for a glass of sherry or vermouth.

At home, the beginner could start with one of these measures, or he could use a $2\frac{1}{2}$-oz cocktail glass as a measure instead, judging thirds, halves, etc. by eye. Measuring does save waste.

Glasses For parties most wine shops, given the party order, lend glasses free. At home I suggest, *as a maximum* for normal needs, twelve of each of the following (the figures are capacities in fl oz): $2\frac{1}{2}$-oz cocktail glasses; 5-oz wine glasses for sherry, port, sours; 5-oz 'flute' glasses for champagne and sparkling wines; 8-oz wine glasses for wine at table; 10-oz tumblers.

EQUIPMENT

Again, the list below is a maximum. Perfectly good cocktails can be made by improvisation. Though a 1-pint shaker (20 fl oz) will make eight cocktails, the quart size, holding more ice, would be better. A quart – rather than a pint – mixing glass may also be preferable. Warm or wishy-washy cocktails are terrible; better too large than too small.

One large shaker with a metal top, though the base may be glass
Measures as above
One large mixing or bar glass, with a lip for pouring
Strainer: Hawthorne type as illustrated on page 19
A long-handled mixing spoon
Ice pick, ice scoop, ice tongs
Lemon squeezer, knife, fork and spoon for fruits
Corkscrew, crown cork opener, champagne bottle stopper, cloths, napkins
An implement for crushing fruit, sugar and mint
Straws and cherry sticks, nutmeg grater, salt, cayenne
Shaker bottles for bitters
Serving trays
Glasses as above

Ingredients Lemons, limes, oranges, cherries, olives, onions, mint, cucumber, cloves, ginger, cinnamon, nutmeg, sugars, salt, celery salt, cayenne, tomato juice and Worcestershire sauce.

Ice Always have enough ice. Spare the ice and spoil the drink should be the barman's motto. For a party at home, anything from a bucket to a tin wash tub suitable for bathing a terrier may be needed, as well as waterproof protection for the carpet.

Suppliers of Equipment The headings 'Bar Fixtures and Fittings' and 'Glassware Suppliers' in the Yellow Pages Classified Telephone Directory should lead to a satisfactory supplier.

STRENGTHS (ALCOHOLIC)

Methods for measuring alcoholic strengths vary from country to country and many people find them difficult enough to understand in their own. However, we can agree that water (no alcohol) can be 0 at the bottom on any scale, and that absolute alcohol will come at the top. Between top and bottom, the scale can be divided into any number of parts, just as a mile can be divided into yards, chains or furlongs. The Americans chose 200 parts; the British, who wanted proof spirit to be 100, chose 175.

Proof spirit had long been regarded as about half and half absolute alcohol and water, before Sikes hydrometer achieved an accurate definition – a liquid, which at $11°C/51°F$ contains 57.06% alcohol by volume. For practical purposes, it was easier to let proof be represented by 100 and to refer to strength as so much under or over proof or so many degrees proof, e.g. 30 under proof = 70° proof = 70/175 parts of pure alcohol. The Excise measured the strength of home-made spirits in this way and the Customs naturally followed suit when demanding duty on imported wines.

Neither 'proof', nor dilution with water were of interest to Europeans, concerned principally with wine. They had adopted a metric scale, that of Gay-Lussac, a French physicist (1778–1850), which fixes absolute alcohol at 100° and measures volume at $15°C/59°F$. A comparison of scales is made below but any number of degrees proof can be converted to degrees metric by dividing by 7/4, e.g. 70° proof = 40° metric.

The Americans also made proof spirit 100 on their scale; but, with 200 divisions, their 'proof' works out at 100/200 or 50% absolute alcohol. Italy and Russia follow France, their volume calculations being based on slightly different temperatures. Germany prefers to ignore volume, measuring in degrees of absolute alcohol by weight.

For wines, the metric (Gay-Lussac) scale is becoming universally adopted and it seems likely that, within the E.E.C., it will soon be used for spirits too. This means that Britain would abandon proof and the Sikes scale, which would be no great loss.

Table IV: Comparison of wine and spirit strengths

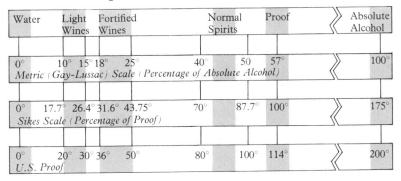

Water	Light Wines	Fortified Wines		Normal Spirits	Proof		Absolute Alcohol
0°	10°	15° 18°	25°	40°	50	57°	100°
Metric (Gay-Lussac) Scale (Percentage of Absolute Alcohol)							
0°	17.7°	26.4° 31.6°	43.75°	70°	87.7°	100°	175°
Sikes Scale (Percentage of Proof)							
0°	20°	30° 36°	50°	80°	100°	114°	200°
U.S. Proof							

THE APERITIF

I know all the Lupinos
I go to their beanos
We start off with cocktails
And end up with Eno's.

Douglas Byng song of the Twenties

SPIRITS

COCKTAIL NOSTALGIA

When my brother, Martin, lived in digs in Cheshire during the Thirties, his landlady, Miss Elliott, seeing yet more empty gin and vermouth bottles outside his sitting-room door, would remind him to order more 'of those aperients as you call them'. Though we laughed, the good lady was not so wrong as may be supposed; both words are derived from the Latin *aperire* – to open, the apéritif being drunk at the beginning, or opening of a meal, with the object of stimulating the appetite.

André Simon, that G.O.M. of the wine trade, whose *Concise Encyclopaedia of Gastronomy* in nine sections, each the size of this book, taught thousands of war-time wives how to cook like French women, was very stern about the apéritif. Neither sweet nor highly alcoholic, it should be sharp, even bitter, in order to alert the taste buds above and the gastric juices below for what they are about to receive, which – in André's case – was usually a series of even more delectable dishes.

In this book, as I am a wine merchant myself and first wrote about wine in André Simon's Wine and Food Society journal, I shall follow in the steps of 'the Master', confining this apéritif chapter of the book to true apéritifs – short, pre-prandial drinks that stimulate the appetite. They subdivide reasonably well into two – spirit apéritifs and wine apéritifs.

Spirits themselves, as I explain later, are as old as the hills; mixing other liquors with them to make apéritifs is a relatively recent development. Vyvyan Holland, second son of Oscar Wilde, who was Vice-President of the British Circle of Wine Writers in the Sixties when his friend André Simon was President, solemnly declared that the oldest mention of the 'cocktail' occurred in the May 13, 1806 issue of an American journal, *The Balance*. The reference, describing the cocktail as an excellent electioneering potion, was to a stimulating liquor composed of spirits, sugar, water and bitters, but there was no suggestion as to how the word originated. This he related in the last book he wrote, *Drink and be Merry*, something as follows:

About the end of the eighteenth century, after some border fighting, an American general met King Axolotl XV of Mexico for a peace conference. Invited by the King to have a drink, the

General accepted as all good American generals do. Thereupon there appeared a glamorous maiden bearing but a single gold cup for the two of them. A protocol quarrel, as to who should drink first, seemed inevitable. Sensing the danger, this intelligent creature proceeded to save the situation by draining the cup herself. Asked who she was, the King pretended the girl was his daughter Coctel, and that chivalrous General, although denied both drink and daughter, declared 'Coctel' should be an honoured name in the U.S. Army for ever more. Thus 'Coctel' became 'Cocktail' and if not exactly honoured, it certainly had its 'whoopee' days in the Speak-Easies of the Prohibition era.

The Times had once called Vyvyan 'a fountain of good stories' and this one must have been a favourite, for he repeated it word for word as an Historical Note in the 1965 paperback edition of the popular *Savoy Cocktail Book*. Far from being a royal personage, Axolotl was, and is, a species of salamander found in Mexican lakes.

There are other stories: of glasses in taverns decorated with cocks' feathers, greeted by Frenchmen with 'Vive le cocktail!'; of a Bordeaux wine cup called *Coquetel*; and a French eccentric who served drinks in egg cups called *Coquetiers*.

If the origin of the word is unknown, Cyril Ray, author of *In a Glass Lightly*, seems to have unearthed the first book, or at least an early one, on cocktails – *How to Mix Drinks, or the Bon Vivant's Companion*, written by Jerry Thomas, a New York bartender, and published there in 1862. The preface, written anonymously, refers to a small drinking saloon established about that time in London, at the back of the Bank of England, which offered 'Connecticut eye-openers', 'Alabama fog-cutters', 'Lightning smashes' and 'Thunderbolt cocktails'.

Respectable as their Queen, Victorian gentlemen and clerks of the City of London were not amused; or if they were, they did not partake. Possibly with names as vigorous as these, they suspected that the Yanks – like Miss Elliott – had got their aperients and apéritifs all mixed up.

Entertaining at home and at official luncheons and dinners, the Victorians and the Edwardians did without apéritifs. As late as 1920 I can just remember dinner guests without a glass assembled in my parents' drawing room amid 'cheerful chintzes patterned with larger cabbage roses on a white ground', a perfect description of '1920-ish' by Osbert Lancaster in *Homes Sweet Homes*. The *mauvais quart d'heure* was later used to describe these dry occasions when no drinks were served.

What could have been served? Gin was 'Mother's Ruin', a common drink drunk in pubs, where respectable women did not venture. Rum was a rude drink for ruder sailors. Scotch whisky, officially, was malt whisky until 1909, when a Royal Commission recognised the blended variety that has since conquered the world. Champagne, relatively expensive, was not regarded as suitable, which left sherry and the dry madeiras as the only possibilities, disregarding hock and seltzer, a cult of the Oscar Wilde set.

I am quite sure myself that the cocktail was an American invention. The United States is for the most part a hot country, as anybody knows who has been to New York in August. Needing cold drinks, Americans have been the inventors of cobblers, coolers, juleps and highballs. Many of them also believe that the purpose of drinking alcohol is to get drunk, which is why ships of the U.S. Navy are dry. I remember a war-time lieutenant saying to a British counterpart, 'In America we drink to get drunk; you British are only interested in seeing how much you can drink *without* getting drunk and, say, that's not logical.'

Short, sharp and strong, the cocktail was just right for the pulsating, 'go-getting' business life of early twentieth-century America, and if at first it was confined to bars and 'Speak-Easies', the cocktail party at home became much more practicable when the domestic refrigerator and Henry Ford's Model 'T' replaced respectively the ice man and Shanks's pony.

On the British side of the Atlantic, Alan Jenkins' delightful book *The Twenties* attributes the fashion to the Bright Young People, immortalised by Evelyn Waugh in *Vile Bodies*. Every generation likes to make its mark, partly to shock its parents, and these Bright Young Things were rich enough to roar around in cars by Austin and Morris on treasure hunts and find-the-hidden-clue parties from Mayfair to Maidenhead.

Born in 1912 I was too young to be even a Bright Young Thing, but with my jovial brother-in-law Jack Paterson to set me an example, transferring my love from a fourpenny fizz called Champagne Ciderette to cocktails, could not be long delayed. The seduction took place in August 1927 at the Riviera Hotel, Maidenhead when (my father, a County Court judge, not being present) Jack stood me a 'Gin and It'. The cherry was delicious.

My father had rented The Vicarage at Bray for the family summer holiday. Twice daily, at 11.30 a.m. and 6 p.m. he would lead an apéritif procession (adults only) through the churchyard to The Hind's Head, the village pub that was later to become a gastronomic shrine for members of André Simon's Wine and Food Society when Barry Neame took it over in the Thirties. The smarter 'High Life' was to be had at The Hotel de Paris (a Thames-side version of London's Café de Paris) from which, in bed after dark, I could hear the mellifluous sounds of Teddy Brown's xylophone floating down the river.

In that summer of fifty years ago, the flips we took were not drinks, but five-shilling flights in a bi-plane from a nearby field. In America the spirit of the moment was 'The Spirit of St. Louis', no drink either but the monoplane in which Lindbergh had just flown the Atlantic solo, from New York to Paris. (As if to symbolise the return of a Pilgrim Father, the cocktail named after Lindbergh was based on Plymouth gin.)

How curious that he should have flown from a land that, having created many of the agreeable drinks in this book, should then have banished them all. Prohibition (known as the Noble Experiment), which made the manufacture, transportation and sale of alcohol illegal, lasted from 1920 to 1933. In the words of Alistair Cooke in his book *America*, 'It opened up green pastures to men who organised their own breweries and transport, paid off the police, supplied rot-gut liquor to hand-picked clubs, and stuck the owners with a further protection fee . . .'

It took thirteen years to concede that the Noble Experiment was a squalid disaster and it remains an outstanding example of how thoughtless, emotional action so often leads to evil far worse than that it seeks to eradicate.

Two more books about cocktails and mixed drinks appeared in London in the Thirties, both by R. de Fleury. His first, published in 1934, was *1700 Cocktails for the Man Behind the Bar*, followed – as if 1700 were not enough – in 1937 by a more ambitious work, *1800 And All That*, of which I have a copy. It is dedicated to 'My friends Messrs. Grierson, Oldham & Co. Ltd., 25 Haymarket S.W.1.'. Founded in 1820, Grierson, Oldham had become leading suppliers of wines and spirits to hotels and restaurants throughout Britain. Among those friends must have been the late Paul Dauthieu, one of their two London representatives until he left in 1939 to start the one Peter Dominic shop in Horsham that was destined to multiply to 400 within fifteen years of my joining the Company in 1956.

Since every barman making a new cocktail, on either side of the Atlantic, gave it some sort of a topical name, Mr. Fleury had no difficulty in reaching four figures. For today's Senior Citizens, running through his list is sheer nostalgia:

Tunes:	*Blue Heaven* (Cointreau, anisette and lemon juice seems to be going it a bit for 'Molly and me and baby makes three'), *Blue Moon, Broadway* (Melody).
Dancing:	*Gigolo, Tango, Rhumba.*
Films:	*Seventh Heaven, Sonny Boy, Hell's Angel, Thin Man.*
Luv:	*Hold Me, Hug Me, Kiss Me Again, Lovers.*
Hope:	*Locarno* (A Peace Treaty), *League of Nations.*
Ships:	*Queen Elizabeth, R.M.S. Queen Mary, Normandie, Noah's Ark.*
Cars:	*Dunlop for the Tyred* (cars *were* pretty funny in those days), *Synchromesh.*
Trains:	*Blue Train, Golden Arrow, Bristolian.*
Sport:	*Googly, Yorker, Holed in One, Three-Quarter, Corinthian* (the great *amateur* soccer club), *Cricketer's Special* (4 parts rum to 1 of whisky, evidently a cold summer at Lord's).

THE BIG SEVEN

In 1929, at the height of the cocktail era, there were believed to be 120 good recipes – as opposed to names, which were legion, because every inventor of a cocktail named it himself and there was little or no international co-ordination. The sixth (1976) edition of that excellent paperback *International Guide to Drinks* gives some 280 recipes, some of them prize-winning entries in cocktail competitions, both national and international, which have been held since the war. André Simon's *A Concise Encyclopaedia of Gastronomy*, Section VIII (the Drink Section), published in 1946, gives recipes and names of 106 cocktails, yet such is the plethora of names that only thirty-five of his appear in the 'International Guide'.

Although Englishmen are said to take their pleasures seriously, I doubt whether the average host, and certainly not the beginner, would want to dabble with more than half a dozen or so. That master of the shaker, David Embury, an American behind the bar comparable to his compatriot Bobby Fischer behind a chessboard, declared in his book *The Fine Art of Mixing Drinks* that there were really no more than six basic cocktails. Here they are, with the White Lady, added by me, making seven.

Martini (gin), White Lady (gin), Manhattan (whiskey), Old Fashioned (whiskey), Daiquiri (rum), Sidecar (brandy), Jack Rose (applejack).

THE MARTINI

The celebrated dry Martini was first made by a New York barman called Martinez, the name subsequently being confused with Martini & Rossi, who make vermouth. Proportions of gin to vermouth vary according to personal taste. The United Kingdom Bartenders' Guild give the original recipe as half gin and half vermouth, adding a note that 3 parts gin to 1 part vermouth should satisfy most British tastes.

In America, where reaction to 1 part gin to 2 parts vermouth is 'wishy-washy', they have gone so far as to reduce the vermouth to a dash, rinse or spray. Experiment as you wish with the best of all apéritif cocktails (2 dashes of orange bitters, an olive, plain or stuffed, these may all be tried), but I'm inclined to think that extremes belong to politics rather than to cocktails, in which case too little gin spoils the Party and too much prevents the Speaker being heard.

Opposite *Mixing glass ; ice bucket and tongs ; shaker ; 12-oz and 8-oz glasses ; lemon squeezer ; long-handled mixing spoon ; corkscrew ; cocktail fork ; 5-oz and 2½-oz glasses ; measures ; Hawthorne strainer*

THE WHITE LADY

After the Martini, the next greatest gin-based cocktail is surely the White Lady – 2 parts gin, 1 part Cointreau and 1 part lemon juice, shaken with a dash of egg white.

My friend, Derek Barrow, likes to tell how he introduced it at Hansellman, the famous cake shop at St. Moritz, when he was Reuter's correspondent there in the Twenties. After a 10 a.m. breakfast at the Palace Hotel, fashionable young ladies, clad in silk ski-ing trousers and mink coats, would spend the first part of the morning choosing jewellery at Cartiers, moving on for coffee or chocolate *mit Schlag* (whipped cream) at Hansellman's about 11.30 a.m. Worn out by such a morning, Derek suggested to Mr. Hansellman that these ladies might prefer a more reviviscent beverage and, since the proprietor confessed that he himself knew little about alcoholic drinks, Derek prescribed a White Lady. The experiment was a huge success; Mr. Hansellman served them to perfection, at a most reasonable price, in tumblers full to the brim. So great was the reviviscence of two such Hansellman White Ladies that Derek, put on the train for England after three farewell parties, remembers coming to down the line from St. Moritz in a third-class compartment, the eyes of five clean-looking, scrupulous Swiss passengers averted, a ticket collector standing over him. Finding his ticket proved to be a nightmare due to a large wooden obstruction hanging from his neck. It was a notice board and the notice in four languages read:
Beware! Danger of Avalanche

THE MANHATTAN

Best known of the whiskey cocktails, the recipe is 2 parts Rye whiskey, 1 part sweet vermouth, a dash of Angostura and a cherry. Take away the Daiquiris and the Old Fashioneds and, says Embury, more Martinis and Manhattans are drunk in this world than all the other 280 kinds of cocktail put together. Rye and Bourbon are preferred to Scotch whisky; sweet vermouth is held to blend better with whiskies than dry.

THE OLD FASHIONED

André Simon, having excluded the Manhattan from his *Concise Encyclopaedia of Gastronomy*, called the Old Fashioned 'one of the most popular and one of the most palate-paralysing forms of cocktails, fashionable in the U.S.A.'. Embury, after declaring it 'a truly magnificent cocktail', says it is 'actually a short highball rather than

Opposite A Selection from The Big Seven: Manhattan (sweet); Jack Rose; Daiquiri; Old Fashioned

a cocktail', which I find about as clear as the sugar syrup essential to its making. Here's how to make the famous 'palate-paralyser':
Pour into each tumbler 1–2 teaspoonfuls of sugar syrup (see page 25) and add 1–3 dashes of Angostura. Stir to blend them. Add a little Rye or Bourbon and stir again. Add two large cubes of ice. Fill the tumbler with more whiskey, nearly to the top. Stir again. Take a twist of lemon and drop it into the glass. Decorate with a maraschino cherry on a cocktail stick. Serve with the stirring implement in the glass. (Without sugar syrup, a lump of sugar can first be dissolved in the glass with lukewarm water.)

A dash of a sweetening liqueur – Curaçao or Cointreau for example – can be added. Bourbon or Rye make the original Old Fashioned theme; other spirits (Scotch whisky, gin, brandy, etc.) may be used in place of Bourbon or Rye to form the variations, without otherwise changing the accompaniment.

THE DAIQUIRI

Properly made, I would argue that this is the best cocktail after the dry Martini. The recipe is 3 parts white rum, 1 part fresh lime (or lemon) juice and 3 dashes gomme syrup (see page 25). The Bacardi cocktail is similar, with Grenadine instead of sugar.

Just rum cocktails to us in the Thirties, the names Bacardi and Daiquiri (not even to be found in R. de Fleury's aforementioned 1937 book) had not yet left Cuba. *Grossman's Guide to Wines, Spirits, and Beers*, an admirable book better known in the United States, tells how, in 1898, American engineers helped develop the Daiquiri iron mines in Santiago, Cuba, where the barman invented the drink for them. Later on, when Charles M. Schwab, their President of Bethlehem Steel paid a call, the *vin d'honneur* was ten bottles of Bacardi Carta Blanca, a pound of sugar, the juice of a hundred limes, two big pails of ice – the lot mixed in, and served from, half an oak barrel.

This emphasises the secret of rum cocktails and longer cold drinks – ice and the juice of fresh limes. Lemon juice – the better of the two with brandy or gin – is no substitute for those gorgeous green limes, never widely on sale in Britain, though sometimes obtainable at a price.

Cuban white rum may be best, but the other brands I mention on page 49 should be satisfactory. Either Falernum, a white syrup, or Orgeat, a non-alcoholic almond-flavoured syrup, both from the Caribbean, are recommended in place of sugar syrup. The Daiquiri being a cloudy cocktail, sherries and olives are better kept to decorate the clear, clean look of a Martini or Manhattan.

THE SIDECAR

After the Daiquiri, the Sidecar reminds me of the sort of changes professional football club managers make part way through the second half. In this case rum goes off and brandy comes on, lemon juice replaces lime and Cointreau becomes the sweetener. But none of your 3 4 3s or 4 4 2s; proportionally this formation does not change, so it is: 3 parts brandy, 1 part lemon juice and 3 dashes of Cointreau (overdo the Cointreau and the drink can be too sweet and sickly).

THE JACK ROSE

This calvados cocktail (applejack cocktail if you can find any apple brandy other than calvados) is really a Sidecar, substituting apple brandy for grape brandy. Grenadine gives it more colour than Cointreau so the recipe becomes: 3 parts calvados, 1 part Grenadine and the juice of $\frac{1}{2}$ a lime or lemon.

The recommended technique is to shake with cubes or crushed ice, straining into frosted cocktail glasses and adding a twist of lemon. To frost glasses, pour a little Grenadine into a saucer, dipping the rims, face down, into it; spin by the stem to remove surplus liquid and then dip in fine sugar.

I once drove from Dieppe to Paris in November into an icy wind that seemed to be blowing from the top of Mont Blanc. The car heater, normally adequate, was impotent, and we stopped at Forges-les-Eaux to drink calvados in front of a roaring fire. The combination was miraculous; for us calvados became 'Eaux-des-Forges' as we drove on very comfortably. Quite the most efficient internal heater I ever drank, the Normans call it *trou normande*, because it 'burns' a large hole in the stomach, which they – lucky people – fill with *sole normande* and *caneton à la Rouennaise*.

ᏠOW ᎢO ᎷᎯᏦᎬ ᏟOᏟᏦᎢᎯᏏᏚ

Making cocktails is a very simple matter of mixing and chilling ingredients, either by stirring them gently with a long spoon in the professional's mixing glass (or in a jug) until the mixture is quite cold; or, by shaking them, vigorously, in a glass or metal shaker.

Shake or Stir?
Any cocktail can be made by either method. It is quicker to shake – five seconds perhaps as opposed to ten – but the cocktail has a cloudy look. Stirring, though slower, is therefore preferred when vermouth or other wines are among the ingredients, because the cocktail will then be given that clear limpid look, much prized in the Martini and the Manhattan.

When, however, citrus juices are present, limpidity is precluded by either method and bartenders use the shaker. A shaker or a mixing glass symbol has been placed alongside each cocktail recipe, but please remember that, whether you shake or you stir, the taste will be the same.

Order of Mixing Ingredients
The shaker or mixing glass is first half-filled with ice. The other ingredients follow in any order. (A professional barman puts the cheapest ingredient in first, solely to save money if the drink is spoilt. For example, his customer could be called to the telephone, the delay diluting a part-made drink.)

Glasses
Being a short appetiser, a cocktail is usually served in a small cocktail glass of capacity $2\frac{1}{2}$ to $3\frac{1}{2}$ oz. The drink will, of course, be quite as good in a larger glass part full.

Ice
Ice is ice whether by the berg, the block or the cube. Crushed ice and shaved ice are professional terms related to machines breaking ice into smaller pieces. Apart from being a little less cold and not quite so clear, ice in cubes from a domestic refrigerator is no different and entirely satisfactory.

The cubes come from the cold compartment at about $-7°C/20°F$ (well below melting point) so that, used without delay, cocktails – stirred or shaken – will be cooled without dilution. If you fancy cracked ice, place cubes in a cloth and break them with a mallet.

One sensible author (inspired perhaps by the Marx Brothers' 'and two hard-boiled eggs'), concluded every recipe with 'and a tub of ice'; it is the quantity that matters.

Chilling
Better cocktails are made if the shaker, the mixing glass and the glasses are chilled in advance. Either leave them in the refrigerator for an hour or rotate a few ice cubes in them for a few seconds.

Frosting Glasses
Frosting glasses has nothing to do with temperature, it is done for appearance, notably in the Daiquiri cocktail. Moisten the rims with a lemon or coloured syrup and then immerse them in fine sugar.

Fruit Juices
Always use freshly squeezed juice from fresh fruits. If the outside skin has lost colour, the juice will not be fresh. Oranges and lemons first soaked in hot water give more juice.

When the recipe requires a twist (or the zest) of orange or lemon peel, squeeze the oil of the peel on top of the cocktail and drop the peel into the glass. Cherries, onions, olives and fruit decor are added *after* pouring out a cocktail, unless otherwise stated.

Syrups
Those sweetening agents, the non-alcoholic syrups, such as Grenadine and Orgeat, should be added before icing any drink; sweet liquors blend best when warm.

To make gomme (sugar) syrup: boil for a few minutes in a saucepan 3 cups of sugar to 1 cup of cold water. Allow to cool and then bottle.

Shakers
The best shakers are in two halves, the base being of metal or glass and the top of metal. Those with a strainer in the top strain too slowly. All the ingredients, including ice, are put in the base, the top fitted to it and the cocktail shaken.

Straining
All cocktails need straining in order to leave the ice behind in the shaker or mixing glass. The Hawthorne type strainer (illustrated on page 19) is used in conjunction with either. Being no longer fresh, the ice should be thrown away.

Temperature
When shaking or stirring, your hand on the metal or glass should

indicate when the drink is cold enough. If in doubt, when making cold drinks of all kinds, keep tasting them.

Method
The method of making every cocktail in this book is the same and to repeat it with every recipe would be extremely boring. The proportions, however, can and should be changed by you, the reader, to suit *your* taste and circumstances. There are times when one feels like a stronger drink than at others. On the other hand, serving very strong drinks to guests driving home is irresponsible.

I advise the beginner to experiment first with ice and water. Half-fill the shaker with ice, then fill the other half with water, using one of the measures given on page 9 (the London barman generally uses a 6-out). This will establish the capacity of the shaker in terms of your measure. Pouring out into the glasses of your choice will establish how many cocktails your shaker will make. The experiment can be repeated to graduate the mixing glass.

Arrangement
The cocktails are grouped under their base spirit or principal ingredient, i.e. gin, whisky, vermouth, etc. The names and proportions given are those used by the United Kingdom Bartenders' Guild and I am grateful for their permission to publish them.

SPIRITS IN GENERAL

Spirits can be made from any raw material containing sugar or starch. Starch, a carbohydrate in the same group as sugar, gums and cellulose and the most widely distributed substance in the vegetable world, is found in cereals, potatoes, lentils, arrowroot, tapioca, yams and sago; when we eat these starchy foods, our alimentary system converts them into soluble sugar.

All germinated grain seeds contain starch. In brewing and distilling the first step is to convert the starch into sugar, the second to obtain a liquid, the third to ferment the liquid with yeast and the last to distil it. The preliminary process of malting consists of wetting the grain and spreading it on a warm floor, so that the seed begins to germinate. Thus the seed prepares to feed the expected plant by converting its starch to sugar or *maltose*.

Next the grain is dried at a higher temperature above a fire – in Scotland a peat fire, which imparts that unique flavour to Scotch whisky. When required, this grain is ground to a *grist* and mixed with hot water in *mash tuns* at controlled temperatures. This process converts the soluble starches in the malt into fermentable sugar in the liquid, which is run off to the fermentation vats after cooling. Fermentation, induced by yeast, converts the *wort* into *wash*, a mildly alcoholic liquid suitable for distilling.

These essential preliminaries and the distilling operation can be seen by visitors at many of the malt whisky distilleries in the Highlands. When making brandy they are unnecessary; fermentation of grape juice has already made the basic liquid – wine. Rum too, distilled from molasses left over after extracting sugar from sugar cane, is relatively simple. Easier still are gin and vodka, the basic requirement being any pure spirit, usually of high strength, from a patent still.

To make gin, the spirit is redistilled at lower strength than the original, in a rectifying still, with the flavouring ingredients added. To make vodka, it is further purified by filtration through hot charcoal, leaving a pure, tasteless spirit.

Distilling itself is as old as the hills. Arrack was being made in India in 800 B.C., and we know that in Wales the mead was so good by A.D. 700 that the bards sang about it. Though there are few early records, I imagine the French achieved their *eau de vie*, the Irish and the Celts their *usquebagh*, the Swedes and the Russians their *aquavit* and *wodka*, at much about the same time. Good news travels fast and the discovery of these new 'waters of life' – for that is the meaning of each of these names – must have been very exciting. Not only was the spirit so strong that a ten-goatskin mead-man needed only one goatskin to reach glorious oblivion, but it kept so much better and took up far less space. Moreover, what a great winter warmer it was for the northerners!

To distil wine they had only to heat it in a suitable vessel until it vaporised, leading the vapour along a tube from the spout and cooling it, so that it condensed to form a spirit containing much of the flavour of the wine. Though early stills were primitive, the pot still, in use to this day, can be regarded as a huge copper kettle from which the rising vapour is led to a condenser, essentially just a tube encased by a water jacket. When cooled the vapour falls as spirit into a spirit receiver.

Wine is roughly 90% water and 10% alcohol. Distilling is possible because alcohol boils at 78.3°C/141°F and water at 100°C/212°F. Wine heated at 78°C/140.4°F gives off a vapour that is a mixture of alcohol and water, the proportion of alcohol being higher than it was in the wine. (In Cognac, for example, the wine's 8% alcohol rises to 20% in the main distillate and when redistilled some of the run reaches 60%.)

In the English-speaking world no great change – no 'break-through' in distilling – occurred until 1832 when Aenas Coffey of Dublin invented the patent or continuous still, one of which will do the job, in one continuous process, of eight pot stills. Far from being continuous, the pot still has to be cleaned and refilled between one operation and the next. The spirit made by the patent still is of very high strength and thus, being so much closer to pure alcohol, it is colourless and sometimes odourless and tasteless.

Happily we make the most of both stills. As I hope succeeding chapters will show, the patent still is admirable for neutral spirits like gin and vodka, which are made palatable by extraneous flavourings. It is used also for white rum, but for dark Jamaica rum and for cognac, in which those salt and mineral 'impurities' collectively called congenerics dictate the whole character, the pot still is paramount. With the best combination of all, a blend of malt and grain whiskies, made respectively in pot stills in the Highlands and patent stills in the Low – by joining, as it were, the high road and the low road – the Scots have gone forth from Loch Lomond to conquer the world with an inimitable spirit.

Opposite *Drambuie liqueur ; Rusty Nail cocktail*

GIN

Don't tell my mother I'm living in sin,
Don't let the old folks know.
Don't tell my twin that I breakfast on gin
He'd never survive the blow.

A. P. Herbert

Hearing that I spent the first half of my working life in the Royal Navy, editors usually say, 'You must know all about gin'. Trying to convince myself that they exaggerate the part played by pre-prandial Plymouth in the activities of the Senior Service, I start counting all the teetotal admirals I have known. Alas, there are not even enough to form a dinghy's crew. There was even one of whom it was said, 'Stick a Gordon's label on his chest and you could sell him for 5s 9d' (the price of a duty free bottle in those far away, halcyon days).

Despised hitherto by the social élite, gin climbed to respectability up the stem of the cocktail glass during the Twenties. It had long been the poor man's spirit in England and a great solace it was to him – and his wife – in the miserable living conditions of the nineteenth century.

Begun by the Dutch as a distillation of rye flavoured with juniper, gin is still sometimes called Hollands and the term 'Dutch courage' was, perhaps, first coined by the Black Prince's troops. Genever, yet another name, is a corruption of *genièvre* or *junever*, French and Dutch respectively for juniper. Our word 'gin' was contracted from it, probably about 1650, when the Worshipful Company of Distillers was formed in London.

Until the accession of William and Mary in 1689 and the ensuing war with France that curtailed imports of brandy, these distillers must have been on part-time work.

Then the rot – later immortalised in Hogarth's 'Gin Lane' – really started. First, patriotism turned every London citizen into a gin drinker, increasing consumption tenfold in forty years. Little seems to be known about the strength or quality of the gin except that Queen Anne had inexplicably ended control by the Distillers, putting much impure spirit on the market; thus, with the masses more or less permanently drunk, the pendulum swung towards a state approaching prohibition. The Gin Act of 1733, forbidding retail sales of less than two gallons, virtually prohibited it to the poor, with even worse consequences. There were riots. New illicit brands appeared under

Preceding pages Gin cocktails: Negroni; Blue Jacket; Alaska; Fallen Angel

Opposite Rum cocktails: Deansgate; Daiquiri Blossom

33

such appealing names as 'My Lady's Eyewater', 'Cuckold's Comfort' and 'Old Tom'. The last named was marketed by a Captain Bradstreet, who was in fact a Government official employed to enforce the Act. The ingenious Captain even invented the first slot machine in the shape of a cat, to which one whispered 'Puss! Give me a gin!' and Puss readily complied.

When the Act was repealed in 1742, our worthy legislators left it to a respected distiller to draft a better one. Thenceforward, revenue duty was levied on the manufacturer and retail licences came under the magistrates, an arrangement still operating to this day.

By Victorian times the distillers – though not their products – were all accepted socially. Sir Felix Booth, grandson of the founder of Booths which had expanded steadily, was a friend of William IV. He is rightly remembered for financing the Ross expedition, which failed to find the North-West passage, returning when hope had been abandoned, having added the magnetic pole and 'Boothia' to Britain's Canadian possessions.

As spirits go, gin is not highly esteemed, because it has little in its own right. With brandy, whisky or rum, the flavour – in greater or lesser degree – is derived from the grape, the malt or the sugar cane. But gin is just alcohol, made from any source of sugar, tasteless until redistilled with juniper berries, coriander seeds, angelica roots, calamus, cardamom seeds and orris powder, to name the principal flavouring ingredients. The complete list always reminds me of my Aunt Grace's herbal therapy days (dandelion and rhubarb laxative pills) so that it remains a miracle how gin can taste so agreeable.

In practice the basic alcohol is distilled from maize and barley, redistilled twice with the flavouring ingredients and weakened by adding water. The strength is 84° proof for Export and 70° proof at home.

The difference in flavour between brands is brought about by different combinations of the flavouring ingredients. Until about a hundred years ago the spirit (like Dutch gin) was sweetened, the last of such brands in Britain being 'Old Tom', still made in London and drunk in cold places such as Finland. The new unsweetened replacement was found to go very nicely out east with Indian tonic water, and in the Navy with plain water, lime juice (a gimlet) or Angostura (a pink gin). Plymouth gin, some say, combines best with water, which may have helped to establish it so firmly as the wardroom apéritif in the days of sail and limited stowage, though in my time its use was not exactly restricted to that one sharp apéritif necessary to alert the tastebuds for delectable corned beef and carrots.

Gradually, from about 1880, gin became drier and less pungent, developing to the style we know as 'London dry', now made under licence in numerous countries abroad – by Booths and Burroughs, Tanqueray Gordon, Gilbeys and other British distillers.

Lacking character does not preclude a person from being a good mixer, and gin – a better mixer than other spirits – follows the human trait. For cocktails and cobblers, fizzes and flips, London gin is ideal; nor do I recollect seeing any discontented faces when tonic, lemon, lime, ginger beer or just plain water are added to it.

The sixth (1976) edition of the U.K.B.G. *International Guide to Drinks* gives recipes of ninety-seven gin-based apéritifs and another five based on sloe gin. I have included over forty in my list, following their recipes which are as authoritative as any.

GIN-BASED COCKTAILS

= Shaker   = Mixing Glass

A.1.

Shake together 2 parts gin, 1 part Grand Marnier, a dash of lemon juice and a dash of Grenadine.

ALASKA

Shake together 3 parts gin and 1 part yellow Chartreuse.

AURUM

Mix 1 part gin with 1 part Aurum and 2 parts sweet vermouth.

BARTENDER

Mix 1 part gin with 1 part sherry, 1 part dry vermouth, 1 part Dubonnet and a dash of Grand Marnier.

BERMUDIANA ROSE

Shake together 2 parts gin, 1 part apricot brandy, 1 part Grenadine and 1 part lemon juice.

BLUE LADY 🍸

Shake together 1 part gin, 2 parts blue Curaçao, 1 part lemon juice and a dash of white of egg.

BLUE JACKET 🥃

Mix 1 part gin with 1 part blue Curaçao and a dash of orange bitters. A mixing glass is used to give a clearer blue.

BLUE RIBAND 🥃

Mix 2 parts gin with 2 parts white Curaçao and 1 part blue Curaçao. The 'Blue Riband' was awarded to the liner making the fastest Atlantic crossing; variously held by British, French, German and U.S. ships, this cocktail must have originated in one of them.

BRONX 🍸

Shake together 3 parts gin, 1 part dry vermouth, 1 part sweet vermouth and 1 part fresh orange juice. Accredited to Johnny Solon, bartender of the Old Waldorf bar in New York and named after the Bronx Zoo.

CARUSO 🥃

Mix 1 part gin with 1 part dry vermouth and 1 part green crème de menthe.

CLOVER CLUB 🍸

Shake together 2 parts gin, 1 part Grenadine, the juice of $\frac{1}{2}$ a lemon or lime and the white of an egg. Serve in a 5-oz glass or larger.

DUBONNET 🥃

Mix 1 part gin with 1 part Dubonnet and add a twist of lemon peel.

FALLEN ANGEL 🍸

Shake together 3 parts gin, 1 part lemon juice, 2 dashes of green crème de menthe and a dash of Angostura.

GIBSON 🥃

An extra dry Martini (see below) with a cocktail onion in place of an olive.

GIMLET 🥃

Mix 2 parts gin with 1 part lime juice cordial. Add water or soda if desired.

GIN AND IT

Unshaken; combine 1 part gin and 1 part sweet vermouth in a cocktail glass. Add a cherry.

HAVANA 🍶

Shake together 1 part gin, 1 part Swedish Punch, 2 parts apricot brandy and a dash of lemon juice.

MAIDEN'S PRAYER 🍶

Shake together 3 parts gin, 3 parts Cointreau and 1 part orange juice.

MAINBRACE 🍶

Shake together 1 part gin, 1 part Cointreau and 1 part grapefruit juice. This is almost a White Lady (see page 39), with grapefruit juice replacing the lemon juice.

MARTINI (DRY) 🥃

Mix 1 part gin with 1 part dry vermouth and add a dash of orange bitters (optional). Squeeze zest of lemon peel over the cocktail and, optionally, add an olive.

MARTINI (MEDIUM) 🥃

Mix 4 parts gin with 1 part dry vermouth and 1 part sweet vermouth.

MARTINI (SWEET) 🥃

Mix 2 parts gin with 1 part sweet vermouth and add a cherry.

MILLION DOLLAR

Shake together 2 parts gin, 1 part sweet vermouth, the white of an egg, 1 teaspoonful of Grenadine and 1 teaspoonful of pineapple juice.

MONKEY GLAND

Shake together 3 parts gin, 2 parts orange juice, 2 dashes of Pastis and 2 dashes of Grenadine.

NEGRONI

Combine in a glass, 1 part gin, 1 part sweet vermouth and 1 part Campari. Add ice, $\frac{1}{2}$ slice of orange and soda (optional).

OLD ETONIAN

Mix 1 part gin with 1 part Lillet, 2 dashes of orange bitters, and 2 dashes of crème de noyau. Add a twist of orange peel.

OPERA

Mix 4 parts gin with 1 part Dubonnet and 1 part maraschino. Add a twist of orange peel.

PERFECT LADY

Shake together 2 parts gin, 1 part peach brandy, 1 part lemon juice and the white of an egg.

PICCADILLY

Mix 2 parts gin with 1 part dry vermouth, a dash of Pastis and a dash of Grenadine.

PINK LADY

Shake together 4 parts gin with 1 part Grenadine and the white of an egg.

PRINCETON

Mix 2 parts gin with 1 part port wine and a dash of orange bitters. Add a twist of lemon peel.

QUEENS 🍸

Shake together 1 part gin, 1 part dry vermouth, 1 part sweet vermouth and 1 part pineapple juice.

R.A.C. 🥃

Mix 2 parts gin with 1 part dry vermouth, 1 part sweet vermouth, a dash of orange bitters and a dash of Grenadine. Add a cherry and a twist of orange peel.

SATAN'S WHISKERS 🍸

Shake together 1 part gin, 1 part Grand Marnier, 1 part dry vermouth, 1 part sweet vermouth, 1 part orange juice and a dash of orange bitters.

SILVER JUBILEE 🍸

Shake together 2 parts gin, 2 parts crème de banane and 1 part cream.

TANGO 🍸

Shake together 2 parts gin, 1 part sweet vermouth, 1 part dry vermouth, 2 dashes of orange Curaçao and a dash of orange juice.

TWENTIETH CENTURY 🍸

Shake together 2 parts gin, 1 part Lillet, 1 part crème de cacao and 1 part lemon juice.

WHITE HEATHER 🍸

Shake together 3 parts dry gin, 1 part Cointreau, 1 part pineapple juice and 1 part dry vermouth. Optionally, add a dash of Pastis.

WHITE LADY 🍸

Shake together 2 parts gin, 1 part Cointreau, 1 part lemon juice and a dash of white of egg.

YELLOW DAISY 🍸

Mix 2 parts gin with 1 part dry vermouth and 1 part Grand Marnier.

SLOE GIN

Sloes – the berries of the Black Thorn – can be gathered from British hedgerows to make a gin-based cordial, though buying a bottle of Hawker's Pedlar or Bols sloe gin saves time (ten years probably). Here is a recipe, but be warned – the immediate result is sweet, sticky and cloying. Maturing for ten years transforms it to 'deliciously clean and mellow', as André Simon described it in his *Concise Encyclopaedia of Gastronomy*.

Put 1 gallon sloes, 1 gallon gin, 2½ lb sugar candy and ½ oz bitter almonds in a 2-gallon jar, shake twice a week for 3 months and then strain and bottle.

Three sloe gin cocktails:

FUTURITY 🍸

Mix 1 part sloe gin with 1 part sweet vermouth and 2 dashes of Angostura.

SLOE GIN 🍸

Mix 2 parts sloe gin with 1 part dry vermouth and 1 part sweet vermouth.

STARBOARD LIGHT 🍹

Shake together 2 parts sloe gin with 1 part green crème de menthe and 1 part lemon juice.

Fizzes and Rickeys (see pages 100 and 107) of sloe gin are excellent and, with Bols now challenging the former monopoly of the Pedlar brand, more may be heard of sloe gin drinks. Lemon and orange gin (there was also mulberry) seem to have disappeared.

WHISKY

When the last big bottle's empty and the dawn creeps gray and cold,
And the last clan-tartan's folded and the last damned lie is told;
When they totter down the footpaths in a brave, unbroken line;
To the peril of the passers and the tune of Auld Lang Syne;
You can tell the folk at breakfast as they watch the fearsome sicht:
'They've only been assisting at a braw Scots nicht.'

Will Ogilvie

There is a magic moment for whisky and it occurs not at dawn but about 6 p.m. This is the hour when we return with empty creel from the finest sea trout loch in Scotland after a fourteen-mile walk through peat bogs in a south-westerly gale. Again, it is the hour when we finally drag our feet into the clubhouse after the round which has singularly failed to show that the slice has been cured. The consolation we drink with soda or water on these occasions is not, however, the true and original malt whisky of the Highlands, but a blend of malt and grain whiskies, which the purist can condemn with justice as an adulteration.

From the Highlander's point of view, the trouble started after the 1745 rebellion. Having massacred a thousand of their clansmen at Culloden, the English could then enforce the excise laws, harshly imposed on the whisky which brought solace to the natives, in a land where zero temperatures in winter, and frost even in midsummer, are commonplace. The defiant and embittered Highlanders soon became a band of Pimpernels smuggling their aristocratic whiskies to the Lowlands under the noses of the Chauvelins of the Excise. One pleasing trick, played when the worm of a still wore out, was to report the discovery of an illicit still, for which there was a £5 reward. The old worm was left as evidence, the other parts set up secretly elsewhere. The £5 came in handy to buy a new worm and start business again.

The battle of wits – and sometimes blows – went on until 1823 when distilling under licence was permitted. Even so, the first to take advantage of the new law had a rough time, being regarded as blacklegs by the smugglers' 'union'. Amongst these was George Smith, who built the only distillery on the river Livet to this day and gave his name to the most famous of all malt whiskies – Smith's Glenlivet.

The whisky of Glenlivet and of some ninety other distilleries in the Highlands and the Scottish western isles is made from malted barley only – in a pot still. Matured in cask for a dozen years it becomes a spirit worthy to place alongside fine cognac, a digestif to be sipped neat, or with only a little water. The fresh local spring water (added to the maltose early in the process to form a liquid to ferment) makes every one of these whiskies different, yet all have a flavour from barley dried over dark peat fires.

For ten to fifteen years after the Second World War, almost the entire output of malt whiskies was needed for blending. Our Scotch 'nightcaps' and 'sundowners' depend upon them for their flavour and character. Now there is a good choice of 'single' malts (unblended products of a single distillery) and names such as Glenfiddich and Knockando (Speyside), Glenmorangie and Dalmore (Ross-shire), Talisker (Skye) and Laphroaig (Islay) have become familiar.

The making of whisky in Georgian times had not been entirely confined to the Highlands. When Margaret Stein married John Haig in Alloa in 1751 and her sister became the wife of John Jameson, later of Dublin, there is no need to guess what was drunk at the receptions. But it was their brother, Robert Stein, who paved the way to both families' fortunes by inventing a new still, later perfected by Aeneas Coffey and still largely used for grain whisky and industrial alcohol today. Thus, in 1832, the distillers found themselves with a machine capable of making as much whisky in a week as a pot still in six months and they looked south at a new potential market – the Englishman, drinking brandy or gin according to his means.

Thenceforward commercial success dictated that, sooner or later, Scotch whisky would be a blend – grain whiskies from the new Coffey's patent still with traditional malt whiskies from the pot still, and the proportion today approximates to 60% grain and 40% malt, enough to impart the inimitable virtues of the latter to the former. The blending – as with most blended beverages – is a considerable art, up to thirty whiskies of different distilleries being 'married' in one standard blend. This style of whisky, which now earns Britain £300 million in exports each year, took almost a century to be widely accepted. In England, at first, whisky was usually rectified and turned into gin. Only after 1880, when the phylloxera insect hit the cognac trade by destroying the vineyards of France, literally at their roots, and the D.C.L. (Distillers' Company) had been formed, did blended whisky progress.

Approved at long last by a Royal Commission in 1909, it only remained for the Walkers, the Dewars, the Buchanans and the D.C.L. (who swallowed these giants one by one after each had gained fame and fortune) to put 'Scotch' into every bar from Banff to Bulawayo between the two World Wars, and to make it the chic drink everywhere after the last one.

With Haigs and Jamesons connected by marriage as early as 1751, it is hardly surprising that Irish whiskey (Irish and American are always spelt with an 'e') has evolved similarly, yet its taste is very different. First, the malted barley is dried over a coal fire (not peat) which imparts no flavour of its own. Secondly, whereas Highland pot still distilleries use wholly malted barley, in Ireland a mixed grist of unmalted cereals – barley, oats, wheat and perhaps a little rye – is added to the malted barley. There are also differences in the stills.

Across the Atlantic, Canadian whisky is made from a mixture of corn (which we call maize) and rye, with 10% malted barley. The rye distillate is made separately and may form from 51% (the legal minimum) to 90% of the blend.

In the United States, whiskey distilling began about 1783 when the War of Independence had interrupted rum supplies, George Washington and Thomas Jefferson being among the early farmer-distillers. The best way to conserve surplus grain in those days was to distil it. The spirit, much in demand as a medicine and a winter warmer, and more easily carried by pack-horse than the grain itself, even became a medium of exchange in parts of the country.

Though Rye is made as in Canada, the more popular American whiskey is Bourbon. Bourbon County, part of the Blue Grass area of Kentucky, abounds in limestone spring water and it was here that a Baptist minister, Elijah Craig, established a still in 1789. In 1835, a Scot, Dr. James Crow, built a distillery and Old Crow remains the oldest Bourbon brand, followed fifty years later by Old Grand-Dad and Old Taylor.

Today, although Kentucky remains the centre of an industry making 60 million cases a year, Bourbon can be distilled elsewhere. United States law merely requires a distillate from a mash containing at least 51% corn (maize to us) at not more than 160 American proof (80% alcohol), to be aged in new charred oak barrels for a minimum of two years.

Bourbon may be 'Straight' or 'Blended' – the latter with other whiskey or neutral spirit.

The longer whisky is aged in the wood (up to twenty years) the better it most certainly becomes. With only ten to fifteen years ageing, Scotch or Irish pot still whiskies, drunk neat or with a little water, rival – and can even be mistaken for – fine cognac. In Britain, standard blends of Scotch and Irish on sale must be at least three years old. De Luxe blends like Haig Dimple, Chivas Regal and the Irish Redbreast, derive their smoother, mellower flavours from spending nine to twelve years in the wood.

In the United States, where their whiskies are bottled in bond after four years, the compulsory use of new casks makes Bourbon mature faster than Rye and Rye faster than Scotch, for which used sherry casks, or used American whiskey casks, are preferred.

Comparisons between all these types of whisky serve no purpose – people should drink what they like and can afford. It can however be said that whisky has too much character to be a good mixer with other forms of liquor, and this is why few worthwhile cocktails are based on it. Even with water or soda, whisky lingers on the palate, 'killing', in my view, any fine wine to follow at table. Scotch whisky for cocktails has the additional disadvantage of the peaty taste and barmen tell me that Rye and Bourbon are better for them. For drinking generally however, American taste has veered away from American whiskey. In 1976, almost 40% of total consumption was imported Scotch, Irish and Canadian.

A fellow wine merchant once told me that having endured agonies from disc trouble he complained to his doctor. 'But you are a wine merchant', said the M.D. 'Drink your own whisky, man, the best pain-killer there is.' Even if I, with Scottish forebears, eschew it for my apéritif, that always seems to be an over-riding reason for never being without a bottle in the cupboard.

WHISKY-BASED COCKTAILS

▉ = Shaker ▉ = Mixing Glass

AFFINITY ▉

Mix 2 parts Scotch whisky with 1 part sweet vermouth and 2 dashes of Angostura.

BARBICAN ▉

Shake together 7 parts Scotch whisky, 1 part Drambuie and 2 parts passionfruit juice.

BOBBY BURNS ▉

Mix 1 part Scotch whisky with 1 part sweet vermouth and 3 dashes of Bénédictine.

BOURBONELLA 🥃

Mix 2 parts Bourbon whiskey with 1 part dry vermouth, 1 part orange Curaçao and a dash of Grenadine.

BROOKLYN 🥃

Mix 1 part Rye whiskey with 1 part sweet vermouth, a dash of maraschino and a dash of Amer Picon.

COMMODORE 🍸

Shake together 4 parts Rye whiskey, 1 part fresh lime juice and 2 dashes of orange bitters. Add sugar to taste.

DANDY 🥃

Mix 1 part Rye whiskey with 1 part Dubonnet, a dash of Angostura and 3 dashes of Cointreau. Add a twist each of orange and lemon peel.

EMBASSY ROYAL 🍸

Shake together 2 parts Bourbon whiskey, 1 part Drambuie, 1 part sweet vermouth and 2 dashes of orange squash.

EMPIRE GLORY 🍸

Shake together 2 parts Rye whiskey, 1 part ginger wine, 1 part lemon juice and 2 dashes of Grenadine.

HOOTS MON 🥃

Mix 2 parts Scotch whisky with 1 part Lillet and 1 part sweet vermouth.

HUNTER 🥃

Mix 2 parts Rye whiskey with 1 part cherry brandy.

INK STREET 🍸

Shake together 1 part Rye whiskey, 1 part lemon juice and 1 part orange juice.

LINSTEAD 🍸

Shake together 1 part Scotch whisky, 1 part sweetened pineapple juice and a dash of Pastis. Add a twist of lemon peel.

MANHATTAN (SWEET) 🥃

Mix 2 parts Rye whiskey with 1 part sweet vermouth and a dash of Angostura. Add a cherry.

MANHATTAN (DRY) 🥃

Substituting dry for sweet vermouth and a twist of lemon peel for the cherry makes a dry Manhattan.

MANHATTAN (MEDIUM) 🥃

Mix 4 parts Rye whiskey with 1 part dry vermouth and 1 part sweet vermouth.

MAPLE LEAF 🍸

Shake together 2 parts Bourbon whiskey, 1 part lemon juice and a teaspoonful of maple syrup.

OLD FASHIONED

Pour into a tumbler 1–2 teaspoonfuls sugar syrup (see page 25) and add 1–3 dashes of Angostura. Stir to blend them. Add a little Rye or Bourbon and stir again. Add 2 large ice cubes. Stir. Fill with more whiskey nearly to the top. Stir. Add zest of lemon to the glass. Decorate with a cherry and serve with a spoon to stir further.

OLD PAL 🥃

Mix 1 part Rye whiskey with 1 part dry vermouth and 1 part Campari.

ROB ROY 🥃

Mix 1 part Scotch whisky with 1 part sweet vermouth and a dash of Angostura. Add a cherry.

RUSTY NAIL

Pour 2 parts Scotch whisky and 1 part Drambuie over ice in an old fashioned glass. Serve with a twist of lemon peel.

SHAMROCK 🍸

Mix 1 part Irish whiskey with 1 part dry vermouth, 3 dashes of green Chartreuse and 3 dashes of green crème de menthe.

WHISKY COCKTAIL 🍸

Mix 4 parts Scotch whisky with 1 part orange Curaçao and 2 dashes of Angostura. Add a cherry.

WHIZZ BANG 🍸

Mix 2 parts Scotch whisky with 1 part dry vermouth, 2 dashes of Pastis, 2 dashes of Grenadine and 2 dashes of orange bitters.

RUM

Fifteen Men on the Dead Man's Chest –
Yo-ho-ho, and a bottle of rum!
Drink and the devil had done for the rest –
Yo-ho-ho, and a bottle of rum!

R. L. Stevenson

'The first thing I saw on waking this morning was a large green lizard hopping about the bedside table. It made me scratch my head a bit until I saw it was a real one.'

The above entry appears in my Midshipman's Journal, which all 'the young gentlemen' were required to write in order to train them in (a) the power of observation and (b) the power of expression. It relates to a morning after a dance, and at least deserves a mark for observation in difficult circumstances. I was nineteen at the time, the date 16th February, 1932, the place Barbados, and the cause of the anxiety as to the reality of the lizard was, I hardly need add, rum.

The British West Indies was then a depressed area; in the spring of 1931 and again in 1932 squadrons of the Home Fleet crossed the Atlantic to raise the Islanders' morale. Whether we were successful in this I do not know, but there is not the slightest doubt that rum cocktails and Planter's Punch did *us* a power of good. The Journal, which had to be produced from time to time for inspection by formidable admirals, refers to these refreshments as 'long cooling drinks'; the truth – 'Returned on board sloshed after a session in the Aquatic Club' – though showing commendable power of expression, was best not recorded by young gentlemen under twenty who, on board, were not even permitted to drink spirits.

I remember being so impressed by the long cooling drinks that I bought a number of miniature bottles of rum and experimented on the passage home to see how they were made. But without success; their secret was the juice of fresh limes and by that time we had none on board.

On this side of the Atlantic, rum has never got over being called 'a hot, hellish and terrible liquor' by some seventeenth-century writer, although there was a brief period on either side of 1800 when it was to be found in the cellars of the gentry. Consequently it has always been treated merely as an effective internal hot-water bottle.

Although this historical spirit was first revealed to the British when Admirals Penn and Venables captured Jamaica in 1655, the Royal

Navy really owes its rum to Columbus, who not only discovered the island in 1494, but took sugar cane cuttings there from the Canaries. Rum had been known to China, Cyprus and Sicily in Roman times, but climate was to make the West Indies the greatest producer.

Whether the name derives from rumbustious behaviour on the Spanish Main or is contracted from what amounts to a double tot in the words *saccharum officinarum* (sugar cane), is debatable.

Writing in *Wine Mine* in 1962, my friend, Captain Harry Barton, declared that the Navy's half pint, issued in two whacks before dinner and supper, was equivalent to having twelve present-day 6-out gins before each meal. Diluted with water in 1740, halved in 1824 and reduced to $2\frac{1}{2}$ oz ($\frac{1}{8}$ pint) in 1850 – which is quite a strong tot at 90° proof – the ration was finally replaced by cans of beer for sailors and commercial spirits for petty officers, on 1st August, 1970. Officers had not been entitled to it since 1850, except on the order 'Splice the Main Brace', a dangerous task in sailing ships, now only given on Royal occasions, or after great victories such as V-E and V-J Days.

In eighteenth-century America, Spanish West Indian rum was so popular that Washington distributed seventy-five gallons among the voters, who not only elected him to the Virginia House of Burgesses but sent him to Congress later. If that was gentle bribery, the rum runners from Cuba to Florida Keys during Prohibition constituted not-so-gentle corruption.

Here, in Britain, consumption declined between the two World Wars from $3\frac{1}{2}$ million proof gallons a year to about half a million. The traditional dark, pungent, heavy-bodied rums of Jamaica and Demerara continue to sell well along the north-eastern coasts of England and Scotland, where winter is no joke; elsewhere, heating in homes and cars must have reduced demand for them. Instead, great efforts have been made to attract the public to the white rums – odourless and almost colourless – which came chiefly from Cuba before Castro took over the Bacardi concern. Bacardi is now made in the Bahamas; other brands are Ronrico from Puerto Rico, Santiago from Guyana, Dry Cane from Barbados and Havana Club, a real Cuban from a new distillery in Havana. These are the rums for cocktails and the 'long cooling iced drinks' like Planter's Punch that taste so good on a white sand beach in Barbados.

The definition of rum as 'a spirit distilled direct from sugar cane products in sugar growing countries' reminds us that, though faithful to our former West Indies, we can accept it too from many South American countries, and from Mauritius, Queensland, Natal, Java and India.

In Barbados, I remember seeing the freshly cut sugar cane being crushed by rollers in the sugar mills. The juice, clarified in large tanks to concentrate the sugar, leaves a thick syrup after surplus water has been drawn off. High speed centrifugal pumps crystallise and separate the sugar, leaving a residue of sugary molasses, useless unless distilled.

Taken to the distillery, adding water and yeast to these molasses forms the wash to ferment, the yeast selected and the time taken governing the final character of the rum. Some will be produced from pot stills, some from patent stills, depending on the locality and the style required. In Haiti and Martinique, the cane juice itself is distilled. Generally sugar caramel provides the colouring and casks already used for spirits are acceptable for ageing. The minimum period is three years.

Rum is superior to vodka, whisky and gin in the sense that, sugar being present already in the cane, no preliminary malting process to convert starch to sugar is necessary. Thus rum retains much more flavour from its origins.

For cocktails, Cuban (light-bodied and white) is best, the white label (Carta Blanca) being drier, better and cheaper than the gold (Carta de Oro). Jamaica rum is certainly the style for long hot drinks, but on long cold drinks I would not like to be dogmatic. Certainly both styles blend beautifully with fruit juices and with most liqueurs, provided there is ice by the bucket.

RUM-BASED COCKTAILS

❦ = Shaker ⊻ = Mixing Glass

BACARDI ❦

Shake together 3 parts white rum, 1 part fresh lime or lemon juice and $\frac{1}{2}$ teaspoonful of Grenadine.

DAIQUIRI ❦

Shake together 3 parts white rum, 1 part juice of a fresh lime (or lemon) and 3 dashes of gomme syrup (see page 25).

DAIQUIRI BLOSSOM 🍸

Shake together 1 part white rum, 1 part fresh orange juice and a dash of maraschino.

DAIQUIRI LIBERAL 🥃

Mix 2 parts white rum with 1 part sweet vermouth and a dash of Amer Picon.

DEANSGATE 🥃

Mix 2 parts white rum with 1 part lime juice cordial and 1 part Drambuie. Add a twist of orange peel.

JAMAICA RUM 🥃

Mix 5 parts dark rum with 1 part gomme syrup (see page 25) and a dash of Angostura.

KNICKERBOCKER SPECIAL 🍸

Shake together 6 parts dark rum, 1 part raspberry syrup, 1 part lemon juice, 1 part orange juice and 1 part orange Curaçao. Add a cube of pineapple.

LITTLE PRINCESS 🥃

Mix 1 part white rum with 1 part sweet vermouth.

MARY PICKFORD 🍸

Shake together 1 part white rum, 1 part unsweetened pineapple juice, a teaspoonful of Grenadine and a dash of maraschino.

NEVADA 🍸

Shake together 2 parts dark rum, 2 parts grapefruit juice, 1 part fresh lime juice and 1 part gomme syrup (see page 25).

NIGHT LIGHT 🍸

Shake together 2 parts white rum, 1 part orange Curaçao and the yolk of an egg. Serve in a 5-oz glass or larger.

PETITE FLEUR 🍸

Shake together 1 part Bacardi rum, 1 part Cointreau and 1 part fresh grapefruit juice.

QUARTER DECK 🥤

Mix 2 parts dark rum with 1 part dry sherry and a dash of lime juice cordial.

SHANGHAI 🍸

Shake together 4 parts dark rum, 1 part Pernod, 3 parts lemon juice and 2 dashes of Grenadine.

SIX BELLS 🍸

Shake together 2 parts dark rum, 1 part orange Curaçao, 1 part fresh lime juice, 2 dashes of Angostura and a teaspoonful of sugar.

SWEET MEMORIES 🍸

Shake together 1 part Bacardi rum, 1 part dry vermouth and 1 part orange Curaçao.

GRAPE BRANDIES
AND FRUIT SPIRITS

'Claret is the liquor for boys; port for men;
but he who aspires to be a hero must drink brandy.'

Boswell's Life of Johnson

I never know quite what Dr. Johnson had in mind by this; presumably that table wine is half the strength of fortified wine, which in turn is half the strength of spirits – still good advice for present drinkers full of 'horse's necks', sitting at the wheels of their horseless carriages full of horsepower.

Almost wherever wine is made, brandy is distilled from wine (by definition from 'the fermented juice of fresh grapes'), and the brandies of Cognac and Armagnac, two regions north and south-east of Bordeaux respectively, surpass all others.

In the seventeenth century, when Bordeaux wines began to eclipse those of Cognac, hitherto shipped to Britain from the port of La Rochelle, the day of the Charentais wine farmers might have ended but for the intervention of a passing Dutch apothecary, who taught them to distil *brandewijn* (burnt wine). Their wine, often over-produced and difficult to keep, had always been harsh and dry so that a new process, which turned ten gallons of poor wine into one of delectable spirit, must have been most welcome.

The Charente-Maritime has remained a province of wine-farmers, each with his own pot still and – with luck – a son to help with the two distillations necessary and the cleaning of the boiler needed between them – a sixteen-hour cycle all told. Though a wine farmer will sell most of the cognac, distilled during the winter, to one of the big shippers, with whom his family has probably dealt for centuries, he will also keep a little for himself to mature in those Limousin oak casks the law prescribes. So doing, he plumps for capital appreciation in cask. With the big shippers frequently wanting cognac of all ages and, of course, paying more the older it gets, cognac in cask must be a far better hedge against inflation than francs in the La Rochelle Building Society.

Those two distillations in the pot still produce a spirit containing about 70% alcohol and 30% of the finest elements of the wine; and it is these elements or congenerics that give cognac that unsurpassed bouquet and flavour.

On sale in Britain, cognac must be at least four years old. Three star qualities, suitable for cocktails and longer drinks, are about that age. To use older and more expensive cognac for mixed drinks is just vulgar extravagance. V.S.O.P. (Very Special Old Pale) and finer qualities – the greatest liqueurs in the world – exist for reverent sipping in small balloon glasses *after* meals. Likewise *eau de vie de marc, grappa* and other distillations from the residue of wine-making are not apéritifs. (Having said this I recollect old Madame Leyssalles of the Cro-Magnon at Les Eyzies in the Dordogne, recommending V.S.O.P. cognac with her *pâté de foie de canard truffé*. Perhaps she belonged to some '*marc* for breakfast' school; it was certainly not to my taste.)

After forty years, or at most fifty, cognac ceases to improve in cask and, once bottled, neither improves nor deteriorates (so long as the cork lasts – twenty-five years probably). The brandy in *ye olde cobbywebbe bottle*, apt to go at auctions for £50, will be no better than on the day it was bottled. Whether that was in 1970 or 1870 is of small importance, what matters is how long it spent in cask. If the label is still intact, that is what to look for. Lichine's *Encyclopedia of Wines and Spirits* says of so-called 'Napoleon brandy':

'Any brandy kept in barrel since the days of Napoleon would have evaporated, and any kept in bottle would be the same, or perhaps not so good as when it was placed in glass.' In any case, there would be none left.

ARMAGNAC

There is, at any rate in theory, no reason why any cognac-based mixed drink should not be made with armagnac instead. Should the least expensive armagnac cost less than the least expensive cognac, it would be sensible to make a Sidecar cocktail with it. Yet I wonder; Armagnac is drier and more pungent, the flavour could be a little different.

The region, between Bordeaux and Toulouse, has been called the 'land of forgotten brandy' and very pleasant it is to admire the old town of Condom from outside its walls, standing on the bridge across the river Adour. But the big commercial battalions are moving in, with their pot stills (double distillation) ousting the old continuous *alambic armagnacais* (one distillation) for three star armagnac, which represents about a third of the total production.

Principal firms involved in the expansion are Janneau, in which Martell have a strong interest, H. A. Sempe, Marquis de Caussade and the Societé Maillac, based in the splendid old Château Maillac.

Without attempting anything spectacular, they believe there is a future for armagnac's traditional flat-sided *basquaise* bottle.

But brandy does not have to be cognac or armagnac. In my R.N. days I have made good Sidecar cocktails and longer drinks with Cyprus brandy in Alexandria, South African brandy in Durban, Spanish brandy off Cartagena, Italian brandy in Malta and French grape brandy almost everywhere when too broke to afford cognac.

⟨RUIT SPIRITS

There are also many excellent drinks distilled from fruits other than the grape – fruit brandies or, to clarify the distinction better, fruit spirits. Of these the best known to Americans is applejack. That sage of mixed drinking, David Embury (author of *The Fine Art of Mixing Drinks*), gives a score of drinks, short and long, based on applejack, deploring that in the States there is nothing better than patent still applejack, only three to four years old. Calvados, which he rightly acclaims, is twice distilled in pot stills from Normandy cider, the species of apples and the extent of 'the apple-yard' being as defined and demarcated as comparable matters in Cognac. Left for fifteen or more years in oak casks, calvados becomes a liqueur comparable to cognac. For calvados cocktails age is unnecessary; the sweeteners, e.g. orange juice and Cointreau, take care of the flavour.

Highly esteemed, the *dry and colourless* fruit spirits of Alsace are pot-distilled from the fermented mash of apricots, cherries, plums, raspberries, blackberries or pears. Drunk chiefly as digestifs but used in short and long drinks, they must not be confused with the *sweet and coloured* liqueurs from the same fruits, which are fruit juices with which a spirit has been compounded.

Of chief interest to the barman (and the chef) is the pure white kirsch or kirschwasser, distilled in Germany, Alsace and Switzerland from a certain juicy black cherry. And, on the off-chance of a visiting Rumanian, Hungarian, Croat, Slav or Slovene, the perfect barman always keeps a bottle handy (not of Grant's Morella Cherry Brandy as quoted in *Familiar Quotations*) but of slivovitz, that blue plum Yugoslav brandy that is the cure for all ills on the eastern side of the Adriatic.

GRAPE BRANDY COCKTAILS

🍸 = Shaker   🥛 = Mixing Glass

AMERICAN BEAUTY 🍸

Shake together 1 part brandy, 1 part Grenadine, 1 part dry vermouth, 1 part orange juice and a dash of white crème de menthe. Serve in a 5-oz glass or larger, topped with port wine.

BANANA BLISS 🥛

Mix 1 part brandy with 1 part banana liqueur.

BETWEEN-THE-SHEETS 🍸

Shake together 1 part brandy, 1 part white rum, 1 part Cointreau and a dash of lemon juice.

BILLY HAMILTON 🍸

Shake together 1 part brandy, 1 part orange Curaçao, 1 part crème de cacao and the white of an egg.

BOMBAY 🥛

Mix 2 parts brandy with 1 part dry vermouth, 1 part sweet vermouth, a dash of Pastis and 2 dashes of orange Curaçao.

BOSOM CARESSER 🍸

Shake together 2 parts brandy, 1 part orange Curaçao, the yolk of an egg and a teaspoonful of Grenadine. Serve in a 5-oz glass or larger.

BRANDY (1) 🥛

Mix 4 parts brandy with 1 part sweet vermouth and a dash of Angostura.

BRANDY (2) 🥛

Mix 4 parts brandy with 1 part orange Curaçao and 2 dashes of Angostura. Add a cherry.

Opposite *Brandy cocktails: Vanderbilt ; Billy Hamilton*

BRANDY GUMP 🍸

Shake together 1 part brandy, 1 part lemon juice and 2 dashes of Grenadine.

CARNIVAL 🍸

Shake together 1 part brandy, 1 part apricot brandy, 1 part Lillet, a dash of kirsch and a dash of orange juice.

CHAMPS ÉLYSÉES 🍸

Shake together 3 parts brandy, 1 part yellow Chartreuse, 1 part lemon juice and a dash of Angostura.

CLASSIC 🍸

Shake together 3 parts brandy, 1 part fresh lemon juice, 1 part orange Curaçao and 1 part maraschino. Add a twist of lemon peel.

CUBAN 🍸

Shake together 2 parts brandy, 1 part apricot brandy and 1 part fresh lime juice.

DEPTH CHARGE 🍸

Shake together 1 part brandy, 1 part calvados, 2 dashes of Grenadine and 4 dashes of lemon juice.

FERNET 🥃

Mix 1 part brandy with 1 part Fernet-Branca, a dash of Angostura and 2 dashes of gomme syrup (see page 25). Add a twist of lemon peel.

GREEN ROOM 🥃

Mix 1 part brandy with 2 parts dry vermouth and 2 dashes of orange Curaçao.

Opposite Vodka cocktails: Bloody Mary; Balalaika; Barbara

HARVARD 🥃

Mix 1 part brandy with 1 part sweet vermouth, 2 dashes of Angostura and a dash of gomme syrup (see page 25). Add a twist of lemon peel.

HOOPLA 🍸

Shake together 1 part brandy, 1 part Cointreau, 1 part Lillet and 1 part lemon juice.

LEVIATHAN 🍸

Shake together 2 parts brandy, 1 part sweet vermouth and 1 part orange juice.

MONTANA 🥃

Mix 1 part brandy with 1 part dry vermouth, 2 dashes of port, 2 dashes of Angostura and 2 dashes of Anisette.

MORNING GLORY 🍸

Shake together 2 parts brandy, 1 part orange Curaçao, 1 part lemon juice, 2 dashes of Angostura and 2 dashes of Pastis. Add a twist of lemon peel.

SIDECAR 🍸

Shake together 3 parts brandy, 1 part Cointreau and 1 part lemon juice.

THREE MILER 🍸

Shake together 2 parts brandy with 1 part white rum, a dash of lemon juice and a teaspoonful of Grenadine.

T.N.T. 🥃

Mix 2 parts brandy with 1 part orange Curaçao, a dash of Angostura and a dash of Pastis.

WHIP 🍸

Shake together 1 part brandy, 1 part Pastis, 1 part dry vermouth and 1 part Curaçao.

FRUIT SPIRIT COCKTAILS

🍸 = Shaker   🥛 = Mixing Glass

APRICOT BRANDY

HAVANA 🍸

Shake together 2 parts apricot brandy, 1 part gin, 1 part Swedish Punch and a dash of lemon juice.

PLAYMATE 🍸

Shake together 1 part apricot brandy, 1 part brandy, 1 part Grand Marnier, 1 part orange squash, the white of an egg and a dash of Angostura. Add a twist of orange peel.

VALENCIA 🍸

Shake together 2 parts apricot brandy, 1 part orange juice and 4 dashes of orange bitters.

CALVADOS AND APPLEJACK

CALVADOS 🍸

Shake together 2 parts Calvados, 2 parts orange juice, 1 part Cointreau and 1 part orange bitters.

DIKI-DIKI 🍸

Shake together 4 parts Calvados, 1 part Swedish Punch and 1 part grapefruit juice.

LIBERTY 🥛

Mix 2 parts applejack brandy with 1 part white rum and a dash of gomme syrup (see page 25).

JACK-IN-THE-BOX 🍸

Shake together 1 part applejack brandy, 1 part pineapple juice and a dash of Angostura.

JACK ROSE 🍸

Shake together 3 parts Calvados, 1 part Grenadine and the juice of $\frac{1}{2}$ a lime or lemon.

CHERRY BRANDY

CHERRY BLOSSOM 🍸

Shake together 3 parts cherry brandy, 2 parts brandy and a dash each of lemon juice, Grenadine and orange Curaçao.

ROSE 🥤

Mix 1 part kirsch with 2 parts dry vermouth and a teaspoonful of rose syrup. Add a cherry.

VANDERBILT 🥤

Mix 1 part cherry brandy with 1 part brandy, 2 dashes of Angostura and 2 dashes of gomme syrup (see page 25). Serve with a cherry and a twist of lemon peel.

VODKA

In the early 1950s I remember reading an article by a British colonel on being a guest of the Russian garrison in Berlin. The vodka was drunk neat and in one draught – the traditional Russian manner – with the caviar before dinner, and, at dinner, for toast after toast. At the end, pleased that he was still sober enough to climb the great staircase to his bedroom, the colonel felt relieved. With the ordeal over and British reputation untarnished, he would be away in his staff car at 9 a.m.

But at 8 a.m. he descended to find, to his dismay, the great mess tables laid just as they had been for the banquet the night before, with a hundred young officers in their same places standing behind their chairs awaiting the arrival of the seniors. To his consternation the banquet was repeated, course after course, glass for glass. At long last, his hosts called for his car. But it was no good; in the Russian sergeants' mess, his chauffeur had been 'sewn up' completely.

This, in the Fifties, being the Western image of vodka, it is nothing short of incredible that in the United States, only twenty years later, a traditionally Russian tipple should have grown from nothing to the most popular of all spirits. In 1975, sales of 27 million cases meant that one in every five bottles of spirit drunk in the U.S.A. was vodka.

This fashion is said to have been started accidentally in a tavern in Los Angeles named, appropriately perhaps, *The Cock'n Bull*. Wondering how he was to sell a load of ginger beer to his local hard liquor clientele, the owner laced it well with vodka and called his new drink the Moscow Mule. Evidently it had such a kick that in no time there was a cocktail too, the Bloody Mary; just vodka with tomato juice, adding Worcestershire sauce, celery salt, pepper and lemon juice according to choice.

In Britain we drink about 25 million cases of spirits a year, this total dividing roughly into Scotch whisky 15, gin 4, rum 1, brandy 2 and vodka 3. But vodka is the only one of these five that is steadily increasing its share of the whole.

The paradox of this situation is that vodka – the most neutral of spirits – is colourless, odourless and tasteless; so much so that a Polish brand has been doing well with an advertising slogan 'Vodka *with* taste', though it must be made in precisely the same way as other brands. Smell or no smell, vodka is succeeding because, even better than gin, it mixes with other drinks. Gin and vodka are the two neutral spirits, first distilled in patent (continuous) stills at very high strength, which makes them tasteless. With gin, a further distillation process of rectification introduces the flavouring ingredients and reduces the strength. With vodka it is the customer at home, or in the public bar, who chooses the flavouring ingredients, adding them himself.

Many people, it seems, do not really care much for the taste of brandy, whisky, rum and gin. The younger generation particularly – men and women in their twenties and thirties, earning well and entertaining a little, taking a cautious drink in the pub occasionally without risking the breathalyser going home – these are the vodka drinkers. And, says one survey, vodka with lime is the most popular short drink, though this may be because it costs less than its rival, white rum and Coca-Cola.

While we Westerners are busy mixing this *wodka*, or 'little water of life' as the Russians affectionately named it, they continue to down it neat and cold in small (liqueur size) glasses with the caviar. Impracticable for us, we can try it instead with smoked mackerel or salted fish, as the Scandinavians do with schnapps and (yet another 'water of life') acquavit.

The basis of vodka, popularly believed to be potatoes, is more likely to be grain, wine or molasses. All the manufacturer needs is a sufficiently pure and inexpensive spirit, which in Europe may well come from South Africa. A process of filtration, passing it through activated charcoal, is then usual to remove oils and congenerics, those impurities imparting character to wines and spirits, yet believed responsible, by drinkers rather than men of science, for the hangover.

After the Second World War, the Russian emigré firm of Smirnoff, first established in Paris after the 1914 war, was bought by Heublein, an American firm, which began to produce Smirnoff in Connecticut. Subsequently made in England by International Distillers and Vintners under licence, Smirnoff has become the leading brand in both countries. There are now three strengths: White label 65.5° proof, Silver label 75° proof and Blue label 80° proof. Other well-known British brands are Cossack, Romanoff and Vladivar. An increasingly popular vodka is the genuine Russian Stolichnaya.

Wyborowa, also with a choice of strengths, is Polish made; 87° Starka is another, based on rye and aged in cask to a light straw colour. Also Polish are two flavoured vodkas, Jarzebiak with rowan berries and Zubrowka from a grass of that name which gives it a herb flavour.

Lastly from the Poles there is Plain Spirit Polmos, a 140° proof vodka, only 35° short of being pure alcohol. I am told the 'do it yourself' wine makers find it very handy.

VODKA-BASED COCKTAILS

This list is short because when cocktails were fashionable vodka – if considered at all – was a tipple for Volga boatmen. Provided you appreciate that the taste must come from other ingredients, then substitute vodka for gin, as you please, in the gin-based list. On the whole I think that vodka, combining so well with minerals and fruit juices, makes better long drinks than short.

▓ = Shaker   ▓ = Mixing Glass

BALALAIKA ▓

Shake together 1 part vodka, 1 part Cointreau and 1 part lemon juice. (A weak Sidecar with vodka replacing brandy.)

BARBARA ▓

Shake together 2 parts vodka, 1 part crème de cacao and 1 part fresh cream.

BLENHEIM ▓

Shake together 2 parts vodka, 1 part Tia Maria and 1 part fresh orange juice.

BLOODY MARY ▓

Shake together 1 part vodka, 2 dashes of Worcestershire sauce and 2 dashes of lemon juice. Top with tomato juice and add pepper and celery salt to taste. Serve in a medium-size glass.

COSSACK ▓

Shake together 1 part vodka, 1 part cognac and 1 part lime juice with gomme syrup (see page 25).

GIPSY ▓

Shake together 2 parts vodka, 1 part Bénédictine and a dash of Angostura.

GOLDEN TANG 🍸

Shake together 4 parts vodka, 2 parts Strega, 1 part crème de banane and 1 part orange squash. Add a cherry.

I am reminded that my niece, Jacqueline Catala, when a courier on a marathon continental tour, swore by Strega. It cured travel sickness on the coach and revived many an old lady for that last cultural lap from Rome to Florence. Strega means 'witch'. If plain Strega does not cast the magic spell, couriers all, try this:

HARVEY WALLBANGER 🍸

Shake together 1 part vodka and 2 parts orange juice. Strain on to ice in a highball glass. Float two teaspoonfuls of Galliano liqueur on top. Serve with straws or a slice of orange. (According to the publicity men, Harvey was a Californian surfer who won a prize. Celebrating too well, he staggered from bar to bar, banging his board from wall to wall.)

SCREWDRIVER 🍸

Shake together 2 parts vodka, 1 part orange juice and 1 part powdered sugar.

VODKATINI 🥛

Mix 2 parts vodka with 1 part dry vermouth and add a twist of lemon peel. As the name implies, this is a variation of the dry Martini, vodka replacing gin. The vodka/vermouth proportions may be varied endlessly.

OTHER SPIRITS

Usual British strengths are given in degrees proof.

Absinthe A spirit infused with aniseed and wormwood, popular in Western Europe until thought harmful to potency and mental stability and banned, except in Spain. Anis, developed instead from the star anise plant, contains no wormwood and has largely replaced it as an apéritif and liqueur.

Amer Picon 47° A French brand of apéritif-cordial or bitters, often drunk with Grenadine or Cassis and iced water. Blends with vermouth, Italian in particular.

Akvavit, Aquavit 79° The Scandinavian 'water of life', highly rectified and distilled from grain or potatoes. Drunk avidly with *smörgåsbord*, really cold in iced glasses, by countless Norwegians and Swedes. Taffel Aalborg is a Danish brand, flavoured with caraway seed (see also schnapps).

Angostura 78° Best known brand of bitters (q.v.), a few drops being used to flavour apéritifs and longer drinks. Originally the invention of the Frenchman Dr. Siegert, in Venezuela circa 1825, to combat disease among Bolivar's troops, it is now compounded in Trinidad.

Arrack A coarse spirit distilled from palms, rice and – for all I know – puppy dogs' tails. André Simon, in *A Concise Encyclopaedia of Gastronomy*, declared that some is much worse than others and none is pleasing to the palate.

Bitters The collective name for a variety of alcoholic tinctures made from bitter roots and barks. The imbiber adds a few drops to his gin or sherry from a 'shaker bottle' and the barman may do likewise to his shaker or mixing glass. Famous distillers of bitters include Abbotts of Baltimore and Boonekamp of Holland; others are mentioned in the course of these notes.

Campari 42° A bitter-sweet Italian apéritif of spirit and wines, named after its inventor; drunk with soda, straight or with sweet vermouth (Americano).

Dutch Gin 70° Variously known as Genever or Jenever (meaning juniper), Hollands, Old Schiedam (where it is made) and Square Face (from the shape of the bottle), Dutch gin is a highly superior product. Made in much the same way as malt whisky, fermentation and triple distillation in pot stills give a spirit the Dutch call *moutwijn*, which then goes on to the rectifiers, notably Bols, Fockink and De Kuyper, who add the juniper and other flavourings to their different specifications. Not ideal for cocktails, Dutch gin is best served cool or cold with water, preferably with an accompaniment of smoked salmon, eel or herring.

Fernet-Branca 78° The best known Italian bitters. Half Fernet-Branca, half cognac, with a dash of Angostura and gomme syrup, make a Fernet cocktail, which becomes a Fernet Menthe with crème de menthe instead of cognac. Fernet-Branca also mixes well if shaken with ice and sweet vermouth.

Ferro-China 36° Felice Bisleri of Milan was the creator in 1881 of this eupeptic quinine tonic. In London, Edouard Robinson Ltd. are the agents for F. Bisleri & Co.

Mastikha 90° A rather inferior form of ouzo, which used to catch the sailors of the British Mediterranean Fleet unawares in the Greek islands between the wars. A delayed action spirit, men who seemed sober when they returned on board at night, could become incapable next morning after drinking water to cure the after-effects.

Mescal, Mezcal 90° Distilled like tequila (q.v.) from *pulque*, this is a much inferior spirit, chiefly because it originates from an inferior cactus which grows to the south-west of Mexico City.

Orange Bitters 70° Made from the peel of Seville's bitter oranges; much used in flavourings for cocktails and other mixed drinks.

Ouzo 70° The seed-flavoured spirit of Greece, usually drunk in the Pastis manner below. Keep out of the refrigerator because a scale can form if the oil in the aniseed coagulates.

Pastis Ricard 75° Popular aniseed apéritif in France, made by Ricard of Marseille. Usually drunk yellow and cloudy, after allowing 2–3 parts of iced water to drip slowly on to the measure of Pastis.

Peach Bitters 15° Law's well-known low strength brand, distributed by Ellis and Co., wine merchants of Richmond, Surrey; rather more dashes need to be added to a drink than when using Angostura or orange bitters.

Pernod 75° In 1797 Dr. Ordinaire, the inventor of absinthe, sold the recipe to Pernod of Pontarlier in the Jura and, until absinthe was banned, this firm was the oldest and largest absinthe distiller. This aniseed apéritif, drunk yellow and cloudy (see Pastis above), has compensated them handsomely.

Pisco A Peruvian brandy distilled from muscat grapes in the regions of Ica, Locumba, Lima and the Sicamba valley.

Schnapps 66.5° In Danish the word means 'a snatch or gasp' such as the uninitiated emit round a Scandinavian table, when raising the small glass amid cries of *Skaal* and downing the lot in one go, as is the custom. Something fishy, such as soused herring, is advised with it, without waiting for the lager and sandwiches, which may or may not follow. Doornkaat (made in Germany) is sold in Britain; Akvavit (q.v.) is another schnapps.

Suze à la Gentiane 35° A tonic apéritif with a gentian and herb base, rather bitter. Drink neat, with gin or with water – and very cold.

Swedish Punch 86° A spicy cordial, based on rum; can be mixed with hot water as a Punch, or drunk neat in small glasses as a liqueur.

Tequila 66.5° The basis of this, mainly Mexican, colourless spirit is *pulque*, an intoxicating beverage fermented from the juice of the cactus, which is variously called the century plant, the agave, American aloe, maguey and mescal. The local custom of a lick of lime and salt from the back of the hand, followed by a neat measure of this liquid fire, may be fine for Hidalgos but not for Hoggs. Distilled in pot stills, the best is aged in oak for up to four years, becoming mellow and golden.

Underberg 84° A German pick-me-up; a miniature bottle topped up with soda water is the dose.

Unicum 73° An internationally known brand of bitters made by the Hungarian firm of Zwack; obtainable in London from F. & E. May Ltd. and G. Belloni and Co., Ltd.

COCKTAILS BASED ON OTHER SPIRITS

🍸 = Shaker 🥤 = Mixing Glass

AMER PICON 🥤

Mix 1 part Amer Picon with 1 part sweet vermouth.

GLAD EYE 🥤

Mix 2 parts Pastis with 1 part peppermint liqueur.

MACARONI 🍸

Shake together 2 parts Pastis and 1 part sweet vermouth.

SUISSESSE 🍸

Shake together 1 part Pastis, 1 part lemon juice and the white of an egg. Strain into a small tumbler and add a splash of soda water.

HAVANA 🍸

Shake together 1 part Swedish Punch, 1 part gin, 2 parts apricot brandy and a dash of lemon juice.

GRAND SLAM 🥤

Mix 2 parts Swedish Punch with 1 part dry vermouth and 1 part sweet vermouth.

TEQUILA 🍸

Shake together 2 parts tequila, 2 parts fresh lime or lemon juice and 1 part Cointreau. Edge rim of glass with salt.

SUNRISE 🍸

Shake together 2 parts tequila, 1 part Galliano liqueur, 1 part crème de banane, 1 part cream, 4 drops of Grenadine and a squeeze of lemon juice.

ʟɪQUEURS

Being digestives, not apéritifs, liqueurs are outside my terms of reference, except in so far as they are used in cocktails and longer mixed drinks. They are mostly spirits, sweetened with sugar syrup, flavoured with fruit, flowers or herbs, some being coloured artificially. In mixed drinks they should be used sparingly for sweetening purposes.

The following include those mentioned in this book, with some added to interest readers wishing to experiment. Usual strengths, as sold in Britain, are given in degrees proof.

Advocaat 26° Low strength custard-coloured cordial from raw egg yolks and brandy. A 'pick-me-up' and relatively inexpensive.

Anisette 44° Sweetened version of Anis; makes a long drink with bitter lemon, ice and a little lime juice.

Apricot Brandy 42° Grape brandy flavoured with apricot. In Britain, if the brandy is under 20% of the spirit content, the name must be changed from 'brandy' to 'liqueur'.

Aurum Triple Sec 67° Italian orange liqueur similar to Cointreau.

Bailey's Original Irish Cream 30° A new liqueur from Dublin; Irish whiskey blended with fresh cream, neutral spirits and a little chocolate.

Bénédictine D.O.M. 73° Very old herb liqueur based on good French brandy; made at Fécamp between Dieppe and Le Havre.

Chartreuse Green 96°, Yellow 70° The only liqueur still made by monks. The green is compounded from 130 herbs collected by the Carthusians in the hills around their monastery at Voiron, in the Jura.

Cherry Brandy 42° Grape brandy flavoured with cherries. Flavours differ according to locality; 20% rule applies as for apricot brandy.

Cointreau Triple Sec 70° A white Curaçao (distillation of orange peel steeped in spirit) still made in Angers, where the Cointreau brothers began in 1849.

Drambuie 70° Scotland's whisky-based liqueur with 25% of the U.K. liqueur market.

Crème de banane 42°, crème de cassis 28°, crème de cacao 42°, crème de menthe 42°. The crèmes are all sweet, the last word indicating the flavour. There are at least ten more besides these four – banana, blackcurrant, cocoa and mint. Green and white crèmes de menthe are the most popular.

Curaçao 52.5° Originally from the Caribbean island of Curaçao; a distillation of oranges steeped in spirit. The blue is merely the white artificially coloured.

Galliano 70° Italian herb liqueur in a tall bottle, cleverly marketed and popular in the United States.

Glayva 70° Blended and sweetened Scotch whiskies; similar liqueur to Drambuie.

Grand Marnier 67° Curaçao made in Cognac with wild oranges.

Irish Mist 65° Honey and Irish whiskey.

Kahlúa 46° Mexican coffee-flavoured liqueur. 1 part Kahlúa mixed with 2 parts vodka makes a 'Black Russian'.

Kümmel 68° Grain spirit distilled with caraway seed. Danish or Dutch nowadays.

Maraschino 45° Sweet cherry liqueur from Yugoslavian sour cherries.

Parfait d'Amour 51° Violet, scented and spiced; useful for colouring.

Peach Brandy 45° Grape brandy flavoured with peaches; 20% rule applies as for apricot brandy.

Royal Mint Chocolate 50° Icy green with bitter mint chocolate flavour.

Southern Comfort 87.7° Oranges and peaches with Bourbon whiskey, originally from New Orleans.

Strega 70° 'A witch' in Italian, Strega comes from barks and herbs in the woods.

Tia Maria 55° From sugar cane and Jamaican coffee.

Van Der Hum 54° South African brandy with Cape tangerines and rum.

WINES

CHAMPAGNE

Brims every glass. Seen through each crystal pane,
In tall straight jets or whirled in spiral twine
The hurrying air-beads to the surface strain,
An April shower of bright inverted rain.

Martin Armstrong

What is the best start to a dinner party, or to a luncheon for that matter? A cold glass of dry champagne, I suggest, thrust into your hand by the host as he greets you.

And the worst? That familiar phrase 'What'll you have?' offered without qualification when there isn't a bottle in sight because your host dispenses drinks from another room. 'What'll you have?', though excellent in pub or bar, where it is evident from the shelves that you can have anything from a Green Goddess to a Parfait d'Amour, just won't do at home. The question, unqualified, does deserve the logical reply 'What have you got?' leading to a string of choices ('Well there's whisky, gin, vodka, sherry . . .') which has to be repeated to one guest after another.

With that cold glass of dry champagne, I may murmur that there is sherry, just in case some guest believes champagne is his allergy. George Delaforce, old friend, fellow wine merchant and a great host, used to declare emphatically that a glass of wine, with no alternatives suggested, was the proper greeting. 'After all', he said, 'at home you don't offer guests a choice of soup *or* smoked salmon.'

The worst a guest can do is to produce from his pocket one of those implements that look like a multi-pronged toothpick, proceeding to 'swizzle' his champagne until the bubbles disappear. This is a social gaffe, which those who aspire to drink champagne should realise, just as those who decide to hunt with the Quorn should shout 'Tally ho!' at the appropriate time, not 'There the foxy bastard goes!', as a wartime anti-submarine ace, who had settled in the shires, is said to have done.

The bubbles in champagne – as conscientious readers of wine writers will know already – are as natural to champagne as scent to the rose, and that saint among monks, Dom Perignon, who discovered the art of making the still wines of Champagne sparkle, turns in his grave (and possibly shouts 'There the bastard goes') every time he sees some sinner removing *his* bubbles with that pernicious tool.

Seeing is believing and the best way to be quite convinced those bubbles *are* natural is to visit Reims or Epernay, where nearly all the big firms hold open house, seven days a week in summer, reduced in winter to working days only.

Unlike still wines, champagne spends no part of its life in cask; its permanent home is the bottle from which we pour it. The natural chalk cellars, extending for miles under the two champagne towns, are the birth places and nurseries of millions of these bottles, stacked there in thousands until they have matured and are deemed fit to confront the thirsty world above and beyond.

The original still wine is a *cuvée* or blend of ten, twelve, sometimes many more, white wines; all, of course, made in the demarcated Champagne region, a hundred miles east of Paris. Some are made from white Chardonnay grapes, others from the red Pinot*. After adding a little sugar and champagne to the *cuvée*, bottling begins early in April, the filled bottles, sealed with a temporary crown cork as in tonic water bottles, being stowed horizontally row upon row. The secondary fermentation, which can take from ten to a hundred days, starts immediately. When complete the added sugar will have been converted to alcohol, raising the strength from 10% to 11% alcohol and the bottle will contain carbonic gas and a brown sediment.

Two to five years of ageing are likely to elapse before the preparation for shipment, the most interesting part of the *Méthode Champenoise,* begins; a process fascinating for visitors.

The bottles, still horizontal, are placed in wooden racks (*pupitres*) for *remuage*, a process of rotating, oscillating and tilting each one by hand at intervals, causing the sediment to slide down to the cork in six to twelve weeks. The bottles will then be vertical. The French, recognising that a *remueur* handling up to 50,000 bottles a day ought to go as mad as Charlie Chaplin in *Modern Times* on the production line with his brace of spanners, take the precaution of making a *remueur* the highest paid man in the cellars.

The *dégorgeur*, who removes the sediment, uncorks a mere 1,500 bottles a day. Still upside down, they reach him on an automated

---

* Grape juice is colourless, the skins impart colour. White wines can be made from red grapes by separating the juice *before* colour is imparted by the skins.

Opposite *Champagne cocktails: Buck's Fizz ; French 75*

line; the necks of the bottles having passed through a freezing mixture, the sediment is now encased in an ice pellet which sticks to the inside of the glass. When the *dégorgeur* puts a bottle upright and removes the temporary cork, out shoots the pellet. A little champagne is also lost, which is replaced by a *dosage* of sugar and the same champagne, the *liqueur d'expédition*. The size of this *dosage* varies, the minimum quantity makes Brut, the driest style; the maximum Doux, the sweetest. Extra Dry, Dry or Sec, Demi-Sec are the intermediaries in rising order of sweetness. The permanent cork, the dressing of the bottle and, ideally, a further rest period of several months, complete this preparation.

Strange to say, the sediment's removal, which makes champagne so clear, clean and wholesome, shortens its life. In 1960 when Khruschev asked specially to include the province in his visit to France, Möet & Chandon gave him an 1893, bottled in April 1894, the month and year of his birth. Möet made this drinkable by carrying out the *dégorgment* shortly before his visit. Those who want to drink champagne over ten years old are recommended to Bollinger R.D., the initials standing for 'Recently Disgorged'. Others will be content with the De Luxe brands, like Dom Perignon and Roëderer Cristal Brut, shipped when seven years old at the least.

Champagne is made and matured in half bottles, imperial pints, bottles and magnums, contents in centilitres being about 37.5, 57, 77 and 154 respectively. It is not matured in quarter bottles, nor in sizes larger than magnums; these are filled by decanting from magnums or bottles, an operation which reduces the life of the wine to some extent.

Quarter bottles are useful for airlines and as gifts for friends in hospital. At home I stick to bottles, finding that any wine left over in a bottle will remain drinkable for several days if sealed with a spring-loaded metal cap (made especially for this purpose) and kept in the refrigerator.

All wine needs clear glass to show its pleasing colour and any normal 5 or 8 oz wine glass is suitable for all sparkling wines. Champagne lovers, however, favour the flute, tall and narrow, cylindrical rather than bowl shaped, which shows the bubbles better and keeps them going longer. A continuous effervescence of small bubbles, rather than a short display of large ones, is the mark of good champagne. The one glass to avoid is the flat, shallow saucer-shaped coupe, beloved of Edwardians and best used for raisins or almonds on a Christmas dinner table. At a crowded wedding reception, one jog of the elbow and this shallow glass is spilt; Moss Bros. trousers may not matter, but down a bridesmaid's dress is a disaster.

Opposite *Dubonnet Royal*

Yet another avoidable hazard is the cork that hits the ceiling as the wine froths down the opener's trousers. The correct way to open a bottle is *to turn the bottle round the cork*. Hold the cork firmly with one hand and turn the base of the bottle with the other. There should be no plop, the cork should be eased out ('with the sigh of a contented woman' declared some rude rascal). Occasionally corks are so tight, I find I need my pair of champagne pliers as well.

Champagne tastes best when our palates, unsullied by the day's eating and drinking, and perhaps smoking, are at *their* best. Whenever I attend management meetings of Peter Dominic's Wine Mine Club, starting at 10.45 a.m., a bottle appears at noon precisely. The effect is magical on meetings; not only does the wine taste better than at any other time, but the agenda moves swiftly to an unexpected conclusion by 1 p.m.

Both vintage and non-vintage champagnes – though ready to drink when shipped – do improve further in bottle; the former for up to ten years, the latter possibly for three or four. Old champagne develops a burnt (*maderisé*) taste. To those who profess to like it, I can only say with Shaw, 'Don't do unto others as you would they would do unto you – their tastes may be different!'

Lest I should be hoisted with my own petard, my last, most painful, duty must be to suggest – for those with tastes different to mine – ways of adulterating my perfect apéritif by adding all manner of lesser beverages to it.

CHAMPAGNE COCKTAILS

In David Embury, a mixed drinks man, I have an ally even stronger in his condemnation of champagne cocktails than André Simon, a wine man. Mr. Embury writes:
    'No true champagne lover would ever commit the sacrilege of polluting a real vintage champagne by dunking even plain sugar – much less bitters – in it.'
He adds that, if you must, the cocktail will be cheaper and just as good with a cheap champagne or a sparkling wine.

There is, in fact, considerable disagreement as to what constitutes a champagne cocktail. The U.K. Bartenders' Guild *International Guide to Drinks* and some recipes add brandy; the majority of my books do not. Embury even has a different name for the brandy version, a Maharajah's Burra Peg.

Perfect Temperatures
Storage 10–12.7°C/50–55°F
Serving 6.6–8.8°C/44–48°F
Chilling Chill quickly, not slowly. Use the coldest part of the refrigerator or a bucket of ice and water.

ALFONSO

Put in a medium size wine glass 1 lump of sugar, 2 dashes of Angostura poured on to the sugar, 1 lump of ice, 1 oz Dubonnet. Fill with iced champagne; add a twist of lemon peel and stir slightly.

BUCK'S FIZZ

Into a tall glass put the juice of an orange. Fill with iced champagne.

CHAMPAGNE COCKTAIL

Put 1 lump of sugar in a champagne flute glass. Saturate with Angostura. Fill with iced champagne and add a slice of orange.

FRENCH 75

Into a tall glass put the juice of half a lemon, 1 teaspoonful of sugar, gin to taste and ice. Fill with champagne.

HAPPY YOUTH

Put 1 oz cherry brandy, juice of 1 orange and 1 lump of sugar in a glass. Balance with champagne.

VALENCIA SMILE

Shake together 2 parts apricot brandy, 1 part orange juice and 4 dashes of orange bitters. Pour into a tumbler and top up with champagne.

OTHER SPARKLING WINES

Every wine district in the world uses some of its grapes to make sparkling wines. Champagne being relatively expensive and sometimes scarce, it is cheering to know that there never need be a shortage of other sparklers.

Although I think they are most useful as the basis of long cool drinks, any dry to medium dry sparkling wines can be substituted for apéritif champagne, alone or in the cocktail recipes I have given.

Sparkling wines also deserve a special mark for being fast workers. All alcohol eases human inhibitions and this is why a crowd of shy, silent strangers at the start of a party are so quickly transformed into a roomful of jolly, relaxed, chattering people so soon after the drinks arrive. For some scientific reason, explained to me but long since forgotten, sparkling wines do this trick quicker than still wines, a discovery people must have made for themselves judging by the astonishing rise in their popularity of late.

E.E.C. articles, now governing their production in Western Europe, include names as follows:

	French	*German*	*Italian*
Sparkling	mousseux	schaumwein	spumante
Semi-sparkling	pétillant	spritzig	frizzante

The best dry sparkling wines from these countries are made by the *méthode champenoise*, the secondary fermentation being in bottle. The worst are just made to sparkle like soda water by injecting still wine with gas. In between, many good wines are made to sparkle quite naturally by *transvasement* and *cuve close*, two methods employing tanks or vats for part of the process.

In France the best *méthode champenoise* sparkling wines are from Anjou, Saumur, Vouvray, Touraine and Montlouis, all districts of the Loire. There is also a wide choice of less expensive brands without geographical appellation, from Germany, Spain and Italy, whose famous sparkler, the sweet Asti Spumante, delightful with dessert, is only recommended as an apéritif if you like crème de menthe for breakfast.

TABLE WINES

Nowadays, the imbibing trend being lighter and longer, there is much to be said for drinking, as an apéritif, any dry white table wine suited to both one's palate and pocket. This is no new practice; in the wine trade for generations we have drunk cool draughts of mosel or mersault, sancerre or soave before meals. Such wines certainly refresh the palate well enough to make a man leap for the potted shrimps when the moment comes. Entertaining at home, a bottle among three to five people passes the usual fifteen to twenty minutes beforehand, and when the first course is fish, it may be convenient to serve a second bottle of the same wine at the table, using the same glasses if needs be.

A particularly pleasant apéritif is a *vin blanc-citron*, a glass of white wine flavoured with lemon syrup, as a pink gin is flavoured with Angostura. Likewise *vin rouge-grenadine* is a red wine sweetened with pomegranate. *Vin blanc-cassis*, as much a cooler as an apéritif, is described under Wine Coolers, page 110.

SHERRY

I drink to myself and one other
And may that one other be she
Who drinks to herself and one other
And may that one other be me.

Anon.

With this fortified wine, half the strength of spirits, there are no vintages, no problems of laying down, no corkscrews to be manipulated. Every bottle is ready to drink and if the Vicar does delay his expected call for three months and only a glass remains in the decanter, it is unlikely to have faded away altogether.

The British (occasionally beaten by the Irish or the Dutch) drink more sherry *per capita* than any other nation; real sherry moreover, which by British law must come only from the demarcated region of Jerez de la Frontera, Spain.

In September each year the Palomino grapes are harvested from the chalky hillsides and taken to modern presses in the bodegas. There the new wine will ferment until December when it is racked into clean casks to begin the curious process of becoming sherry. Early in the new year a peculiar white scum, *mycoderma vini* or 'flor', will appear on the wine's surface in some casks. The 'flor' is an unpredictable act of nature; wine from some vineyards may grow 'flor' for a vintage or two and then cease doing so. Not even experts can tell when it will appear, but they do know that fino wines can only be made from 'flor' sherry.

There are only two basic styles of sherry – fino and oloroso – and *in their natural state* both are dry. Finos remain dry. If sweeter wines are required, some sweet wine, made from Pedro Ximenez grapes dried in the sun, will be blended with oloroso sherries.

Whereas table wines become oxidised in casks not kept fully filled, sherry (a fortified wine) thrives on a good airing. The bodegas are above ground and open to the air; purposely the casks are kept only partially filled. After a year, sometimes longer, all wines are moved to a *criadera* or nursery and then, batch by batch, to a *solera*.

A *solera* is a collection of butts arranged so as to form three or more sets of tiers or 'scales' in which wines of the same type and quality, but of different ages, are fractionally and progressively blended.

To understand the system, imagine a line of forty butts on the floor, with three more scales, each of forty butts, on top, one above the other. Suppose the bottom one contains the oldest wine, the top one the youngest. Two or three times a year the shipper will draw off his requirements from the bottom scale, taking not more than one-third to a half out of each butt during one year. On each occasion the wine is replaced by a similar quantity from the scale above, the top scale being topped up with younger wine taken from the *criadera*.

This game of 'general post' suits sherry; aeration through movement does it good and the new wines soon blend with the old in these *soleras*, most of which were laid down scores of years ago. The well-known brands however – Tio Pepe, Croft Fino, La Ina and so on – are seldom drawn from one *solera* but from several.

Once purchased, the dry sherries (particularly the delicate finos as opposed to the bigger, fuller amontillados) need to be drunk soon. Julian Jeffs, wine writer and expert on sherry, dislikes keeping opened bottles for more than three days, though admitting that, kept in the coolest part of the refrigerator, they still seem all right after a week. (I'm afraid I frequently forget that I have a bottle in my refrigerator; sherry-loving guests, apt to call at infrequent intervals, must receive a bit of a shock.)

All alcohol stimulates the gastric juices and, having roused them before a meal, they need to be placated with a biscuit, olives or some cheese, not left to prowl around the tum like the troops of Midian. Nowhere can this be done better than in the bars of Jerez and Seville. I cannot read this description by Hugh Johnson in *The World Atlas of Wine* without drooling like a basset hound in a heatwave.

'There are little bars in Jerez where the *tapas*, the morsels of food without which no Jerezano puts glass to mouth, constitute a banquet. From olives and cheese to prawns, to raw ham, to peppery little sausages, to lobster claws, to miniature steaks streaked with amber onions, the path of temptation is broad and long. Your little *copita*, a glass no more imposing than an opening tulip, fills and empties with a paler wine, a cooler wine, a more druggingly delicious wine than you have ever tasted. It seems at the same time dry as dust and just teasingly sweet, so that you have to sip again to trace the suggestion of grapes.'

For me it recalls a Christmas trip to Seville. At the Torre d'Oro, hard by the vast Edwardian Alfonso XIII hotel, there were hot prawns in garlic and cool *copitas* of those driest of wines, manzanilla and mon-tilla. A double whack of the *tapas* sufficed as a Christmas day lunch before spending a sunny afternoon walking through the enchanting plazas, patios and alleyways of the Barrio de Santa Cruz, the old residential quarter.

When in Andalusia, my most 'druggingly delicious' apéritif is the pale dry manzanilla, the sherry from Jerez's neighbour, the seaport town of Sanlucar de Barrameda. Matured in the bodegas there, fanned by Atlantic winds, this light fino acquires a unique salty bitter tang, never quite so marked once exported. Indeed, if taken the twenty kilometres across the vineyards to Jerez, within a week manzanilla is likely to become just a Jerez fino and, conversely, a Jerez fino will develop a manzanilla character if taken to Sanlucar.

For a colder climate, as in Britain, the Jerez shippers add a little brandy just before each shipment in bulk and, if the buyer runs his establishment properly, each butt will be left to settle for a month or so before bottling.

Names like Croft, Duff Gordon, Harvey, Sandeman, Williams and Humbert illustrate the part Englishmen and Scotsmen have played in the sherry trade, established so firmly as early as 1585 that Drake was able to sieze 2,900 pipes on one of his Cadiz raids. Their brands, and those of Domecq and Gonzalez Byass, decorate the shelves of every wine shop.

Drink the popular cream sherries as apéritifs if you like them best. Yet the true appetisers belong, not to the olorosos but to the finos, the pale and dry group which includes amontillados, slightly darker, fuller, nutty-flavoured sherries into which some finos develop.

SOUTH AFRICAN SHERRY

Excellent wines, made in the Jerez manner, come from South Africa and currently cost about 10% less than those from Spain.

CYPRUS SHERRY

Hitherto, though highly popular and much cheaper than sherries from Spain and South Africa, those from Cyprus were not in the same class. Now 'flor' sherries, made, in the Jerez manner as explained, are reaching the market. Sold at much the same prices as dry montilla, they may well be a great success.

The cocktail recipes that follow certainly do not need the best sherries.

SHERRY-BASED APERITIFS

🍸 = Shaker 🥃 = Mixing Glass

BAMBOO 🥃

Mix 1 part dry sherry with 1 part dry vermouth and a dash of orange bitters. Add a twist of lemon peel.

BRAZIL 🥃

Mix 1 part dry sherry with 1 part dry vermouth, a dash of Angostura and a dash of Pastis. Add a twist of lemon peel.

CORONATION 🥃

Mix 1 part sherry with 1 part dry vermouth, a dash of maraschino and 2 dashes of orange bitters.

GREENBRIAR 🥃

Mix 2 parts dry sherry with 1 part dry vermouth and a dash of peach bitters. Add a sprig of mint.

SHERRY TWIST 🍸

Shake together 2 parts dry sherry, 2 parts orange juice, 1 part Scotch whisky and 2 dashes of Cointreau.

MONTILLA

Not entitled to be called 'sherry' even though the name 'amontillado' must be derived from it, montilla – from the region of Montilla-Moriles half an hour's drive south of Cordoba – is indistinguishable from sherry except perhaps to local experts. Inland, with no Atlantic breeze, the region is the hottest part of Spain, the long hot summers bringing great sweetness to the Pedro Ximinez grape, cultivated here in preference to the Palomino. Consequently montilla reaches the strength of 16% alcohol (28° proof), strong enough to make unnecessary the Jerez practice of fortifying with a little brandy before shipment.

In this natural state montilla is as dry and delicious as manzanilla, yet lacking that sharp, slightly bitter aftertaste. The medium cream and golden styles on sale in Britain are usually of lower strength, because table wines have been blended with them, to qualify for a lower scale of duty, which reduces the price.

MADEIRA

For this superb wine from the Portuguese island, little bigger than the Isle of Wight, the advertisers could adopt the slogan 'All through the day' with perhaps more justification than 'Right through the meal', used from time to time for brands of champagne, hock and occasionally table wines. There are four styles named after their respective vines.

The two sweet varieties, Malmsey and Bual, are uncommonly agreeable with a slice of dry cake, or good north country parkin, at 11 a.m. or at tea-time; even though their true fame rightly rests on being great dessert wines, ranking with, and living even longer than, vintage port.

The madeira that goes well with the soup, or chilled as an apéritif, is fine dry Sercial. Likewise suitable is Rainwater, a light, medium dry blend of Sercials, Verdelhos or sometimes both, named long ago when the rains poured down on the casks on the quay, where they could lie for weeks awaiting a ship to take them to the United States.

Lastly – for any parts of the day not yet occupied – there is Verdelho, a sort of halfway toll-house looking left towards dry, and right towards sweet; a style correct for aldermen taking turtle soup, said Postgate. And, of course, smuggled home in the hip pocket or 'doggie bag' from the municipal banquet it will make a nightcap with the dry cake when raiding the larder.

All madeiras are made in *solera* much in the manner of sherry. They also undergo a heating (*Estufa*) process giving them a burnt flavour and a dry finish, which some people never manage to like. They are not great mixers and I have no madeira cocktails to suggest.

PORT

White port is made in the same way as red but from white grapes. Much of it is sweet; yet there are some brands – Croft Porto Fino for example – fermented out to make an extra dry apéritif, which I have enjoyed chilled on a hot summer evening among the Douro vines.

There is no heresy, in hot weather, in cooling ruby or tawny port in the refrigerator or in drinking it 'on the rocks'.

PORT-BASED APERITIFS

 = Mixing Glass

PORT WINE

Mix 4 parts ruby port with 1 part brandy. Add a twist of orange peel.

TEMPTER

Mix 1 part ruby port with 1 part apricot liqueur.

VERMOUTH

Usual British strengths are 30/31° proof.

Vermouth is more than a liquid to make gin go further; alone with ice and lemon zest it is a fine, if less potent, apéritif, and one which in no way spoils the palate for wine to come.

The origins go back to the herbalists of Greek and Roman times, whose medicinal potions tasted so vile that they were better concealed in wine. Later on, French monarchs and other omnipotent persons had the sense to accept only *pleasant* additions to their wine. By the sixteenth century the Germans had infused Rhine wine with flowers from the wormwood shrub, to make *wermut wein*, which the Latins called vermouth.

In the year 1886, Antonio Carpano, in Turin, made a discovery. For years he had toiled in his wine laboratory, mixing, boiling and macerating herbs and spices and now he had devised a formula worth trying out, in his bar behind the Stock Exchange, on the unsuspecting bears and bulls who met there to discuss the fortunes of the market. *'Punt e mes'* (point and a half), murmured one of them, new drink in hand; and that, we are told, was how commercial vermouth was born. Punt e Mes, the first commercial brand, now a little out of line with current styles, nevertheless remains a good drink, popular in Italy and liked by a discerning few elsewhere.

Italy's huge vermouth industry grew up round Turin in the next fifty years, those large litre bottles from Cinzano, Martini & Rossi, Gancia and others now being familiar on the shelves of every bar and off-licence.

The first dry vermouth was made about 1813 by a Lyon partnership, Louis Noilly and Claudius Prat, who later moved to Marseille. It was used, so they say, in America to make the first dry Martini cocktail about 1860, a claim Martini & Rossi will hardly dispute, partly because they made no dry vermouth then and partly because, since 1977, they have owned Noilly Prat.

The one great place name for vermouth is Chambéry. Light and dry, Chambéry has its own *appellation d'origine*, a distinction conferred by Government decree in 1932. It must be made in the town of its birth at the foot of Lac du Bourget and is distinguished by local herbs picked from the foothills of the Alps; similar herbs, perhaps, to those gathered at Grenoble for Chartreuse, not far away. This is definitely a vermouth to drink on its own. There is also a charming variation, Chambéryzette, pink from a second maceration with fresh Alpine strawberries. About one part of Chambéryzette to three of vin rosé, topped up with soda makes a good summer cooler.

French and Italian companies may now make both dry and sweet vermouth as well as Bianco, the pale sweet variety. Demand is so great that in a typical Turin installation one press will deliver a thousand gallons of juice from a single pressing of four tons of grapes. The juice passes to brick tanks, where the sediment yielding valuable bi-products is extracted, and on to concrete fermentation tanks. Fermentation, started by specially prepared yeast cultures, lasts fourteen to twenty-one days and the wine spends a further ten days at $-10°C$. After this, they turn on the heat (60–70°C) in a plate pasteuriser, completing the treatment with a diatomaceous earth type filter aid.

The non-scientifically minded may well feel that the wine ('that living thing') has now about 'had it', or at least has reached the dead-but-won't-lie-down condition. But the vermouth makers, it seems, regard the treatment as mere rejuvenation, for, waiting round the corner is another set of large concrete tanks, where the wine is incarcerated for a little gentle ageing.

The vermouth we drink is a blend, three dry wines being blended with a fourth, slightly sweeter and fortified with brandy. The blend is flavoured with forty to fifty herbs, infusions being prepared in a large pot still. Cinchona bark, hyssop, marjoram, elder flowers, gentian and, of course, *wermuth* are among the main contributors.

In Italy the grapes come from Puglia, Sicily and Romagna; in France from the maritime *départments* between Avignon and the Spanish border. Casks may be left to weather for a year, exposure to the sun having the same beneficial effect as the artificial heating of madeira.

The making of this apéritif wine, however, is far from being confined to France and Italy. Argentina, whose *per capita* consumption may hold the vermouth record, consumes 15 million gallons a year, few of them imported. In Buenos Aires, I have read, 5 p.m. to 6 p.m. is known as 'Vermouth Hour'. The United States, mostly in California, makes 10 million gallons. Careful selection and blending maintains consistency, so that there are no *soleras*, no vintages, no rules for making it and no demarcated areas. In short, wherever there are enough wine grapes to spare, there should be enough vermouth.

Modifying agent *par excellence* – found here, there and almost everywhere in the spirit and sherry based cocktail recipes I have already given – I can find no actual vermouth-based cocktail, though with cassis (the blackcurrant syrup) and a dash of soda, dry vermouth comes pretty near to one.

OTHER WINE APERITIFS

Mostly based on vermouth, with individual flavours added, there are many proprietary brands containing quinine, which balances any tendency to be cloying. Like vermouth, they are best drunk cold, with a slice or zest of lemon and a lump or two of ice. Few, if any, of their makers say what they are really made of, preferring to make much ado of the secret formula, old and dying Veuve Twanky gasping it out from the four-poster to her son with her last gulp of her celebrated *Aperitivo Tutto il Mio Occhio*.

Desperate for something to say when completing the first *Wine Mine**, I called them all 'Girls of St. Quinians', headed by Madame Dubonnet, the genial headmistress with the claret complexion. Well bred girls of course, mixing well at the bar with all men of spirit – the Booths and the Beefeaters, the Gordons and the Gilbeys – as the recipes in my spirit chapters already show. The additional ones that follow are some in which the wine apéritif itself predominates and male chauvinists had better skip them accordingly. British strengths are 30/31° proof unless otherwise stated.

Ambassadeur Made by Cusenier of liqueur fame, this is a Midi wine apéritif flavoured with oranges and herbs, including gentian to give a little bitterness.

Aperitivo Rossi Wine-based apéritif by Martini & Rossi.

Byrrh Whether Simon Byrrh, the Pyrenean shepherd, passed on his recipe by sheep is not recorded, but it did fall into the capable hands of Dubonnet-Cinzano-Byrrh, who make the popular drink, from a basis of full-bodied red wine, in a huge installation at Thuir, near Perpignan, open to visitors.

Cap Corse 26° Wines from the northern cape of Corsica flavoured with quinine and herbs.

Dubonnet Maceration of cinchona bark (quinine) with sweet French red wines makes the original 'Italian style' apéritif, to which a second brand, Dubonnet dry, has been added.

***Wine Mine** (A Mine of Wine Information) the magazine-price list I edited for Peter Dominic from 1959 to 1974.

Lillet A light, medium dry apéritif based on white Bordeaux wine, with an infusion of herbs and spices fortified with French brandy. It has been made by Lillet Frères at Podensac, 20 miles south-east of Bordeaux since 1872.

Pineau des Charentes 16.5–22% A sweet apéritif permitted to be made solely by producers of cognac from grapes grown in the demarcated Cognac region. A little young cognac is added to young fresh wine, usually white but may be rosé. Quality is strictly controlled, the seal of a tasting panel being necessary before it leaves the region. Strength (29°–39° proof) approximates to that of fortified wines.

St. Raphaël Popular in France and known world-wide, St. Raphael was first made in 1830 by a blind Frenchman called Jupet, the factory now being at Ivry, on the Seine, fifty miles north-west of Paris. The basis is fortified red wine flavoured with quinine.

Ratafia de Champagne To ratify – from the Latin *rata fiat* – means giving formal consent and is associated with signing treaties. Since every liqueur made by the infusion of fruits steeped in it can be called ratafia, the background is confusing. Many are just home-made cordials, but for sweetness-and-light occasions such as signing treaties, a ratafia of champagne, no less, is needed.

Sake 31° Derived from Osaka, said to make the best, sake is a Japanese rice beer, sweet on the first taste but bitter on the after taste.

MISCELLANEOUS WINE-BASED APERITIFS

🍸 = Shaker   🥃 = Mixing Glass

BYRRH SPECIAL 🥃

Mix 1 part Byrrh with 1 part gin.

BENTLEY 🥃

Mix 1 part Dubonnet with 1 part calvados.

DUBONNET 🥃

Mix 1 part Dubonnet with 1 part gin. Add a twist of lemon peel.

DUBONNET ROYAL 🥃

Mix 2 parts Dubonnet with 1 part gin, 2 dashes of Angostura and 2 dashes of Curaçao. Add a dash of Pastis on top and finish with a cherry.

BARONIAL 🥃

Mix 7 parts Lillet with 3 parts gin, 2 dashes of Angostura and 2 dashes of Cointreau. Add a twist of lemon peel.

BLUE STAR 🍸

Shake together 1 part Lillet, 1 part orange juice, 2 parts gin and 2 parts blue Curaçao.

TIGER LILLET 🥃

Mix 2 parts Lillet with 2 parts Van der Hum, 1 part dry vermouth and 1 part maraschino. Add a twist of orange peel.

Opposite *Martini (dry)*

OLIVES FROM SPAIN

COOLERS

Tho' I never like to make a fuss
Unless a thing is positively shady.
But he never even paid
For a port and lemonade
And you can't do less than that to treat a lady.

Madame Drivelli
'The Circus Girl' Musical Play, 1896
J. J. Tanner & Adrian Ross

Opposite Coolers: Mint Julep ; Singapore Sling ; Crème de Menthe Frappé

In the context of mixed drinks, a cooler is an American name for a number of otherwise nameless drinks made with ice cubes ('on the rocks') in a tall glass. I find it more logical to make coolers a generic term, embracing all beverages – long and short, 'hard' and 'soft' – drunk for the purpose of cooling the imbiber.

This is what I have done in this part of my book, and since everybody seems to have invented a name but me, I have chosen to call the miscellany of unnamed, 'on the rocks' drinks, Rockefellers.

Happily, the majority of my Coolers are reasonably alcoholic, raising the morale as well as lowering the temperature and, having been invented in hot places, they make good use of the fruits the sun has ripened. To quench thirst they must be dry; a little spirit and lemon, with cold water or soda added, is the simplest alcoholic form.

For clarity the different groups are arranged in alphabetical order; nevertheless, any 'serious shaker' who has followed me so far, might perhaps turn first to Sours because they are cocktails, converted by more ice and some soda, into Coolers.

COBBLERS

Cobblers to eat and cobblers to drink,
both as all-American as pie and circus lemonade.

'American Cooks' by the Browns, Cora, Rose and Bob. 1940

A hundred years ago these iced and sweetened long drinks, based on spirits or on wines, were so popular in the United States that a writer, Harry Johnson, described the Sherry Cobbler as, 'without doubt the most popular beverage in this country, with ladies as with gentlemen'. Another 'on the rocks' drink, fine ice goes first into a tumbler, the ingredients following in turn, the base liquor being the last. Mixing is with a bar spoon, decor fruit and mint (straws optional).

Applejack, brandy, gin, rum and Bourbon all 'cobble' well when sweetened with sugar syrup, or, alternatively an apricot, peach or cherry liqueur.

Wines from Tokay to Bordeaux, from Jerez to Oporto, all 'cobble' well too. They are, of course, sweeter than spirits, so ascertain by tasting the degree of sweetness of the wine chosen, adding lemon probably to port or sauternes, and only a little sugar syrup to drier wines.

CHAMPAGNE (OR SPARKLING WINE) COBBLER

Place in a large tumbler 1 tablespoonful of icing sugar, then add a thin paring of lemon and orange peel. Fill one-third full with shaved ice topping up with champagne. Stir with a spoon, garnish with fruit and serve with two straws.

MONONGAHELA COBBLER

As above, substituting rather less Bourbon whiskey for the champagne. Monongahela, a town where the whiskey insurrection convention took place in 1914, is thirty miles south of Pittsburgh, Pennsylvania.

SHERRY COBBLER

Place in a bowl or large jug some pineapple wedges, some slices of lemon, rather more slices of orange and mix well with a cup of sugar and shaved ice. Add a cup of sherry, two cups of cold water and stir well. Serve in goblets.

COLLINS

My name is John Collins, head waiter at Limmer's
Corner of Conduit Street, Hanover Square.
My chief occupation is filling the brimmers
For all the young gentlemen frequenters there.

'Drinks of the World'. Anon. 1892

A refreshing long drink, originally a John Collins was made with Dutch gin and a Tom Collins with Old Tom; nowadays London gin is used for both, making these two gin slings identical. Brandy, rum, Bourbon and Irish whiskey Collins can be made similarly. In American parlance a Collins is a Rickey (q.v.), though every Rickey is not a Collins.

A straw was once popular in London. A London chef, fearing that genteel persons would be shocked by the habit, wrote: 'The act of imbibation through a straw prevents the gluttonous absorption of large and baneful quantities of drink.' He went on to urge them to 'accept the vulgar precept for the sake of its protection against sudden inebriety'. Whether this is scientifically correct, I greatly doubt.

My father-in-law, Arnold Powell, one time Headmaster of Epsom College, was adamant that straw imbibation was *more* intoxicating and was wont to sing a cautionary song which began:
'The prettiest girl I ever saw
Was sucking cider through a straw.'

JOHN/ TOM COLLINS

Mix in a tumbler cracked ice, the juice of 1 lemon, 1 teaspoonful of fine sugar and a measure of gin. Fill with soda, stir and serve with a slice of lemon.

CORDIALS

From the Latin *cor* (the heart), cordials – which are sweetened and aromatised spirits – were regarded as heart stimulants. Aniseed, cloves, cinnamon, blackcurrant (all good mixers with spirits), borage (best with brandy) and rum shrub cordials are sold in many British off-licences, the spices, cloves and cinnamon being essential ingredients of many hot drinks.

LIME JUICE CORDIAL

This can be home-made in proportions of 4 oz sugar, 16 oz syrup, 16 oz crude lime juice and 28 oz water. Colour with liquid saffron and filter to clarify.

BRANDY SHRUB

Mix the rind of 2 lemons and the juice of 5 lemons with 2 bottles brandy. Cover for 3 days. Add 1 bottle sherry and 1 lb sugar, run it through a jelly bag and bottle.

CRUSTAS, DAISIES AND FIXES

American terms of unknown origin, these drinks are virtually all Sours (see page 109), served in big glasses (old fashioned or goblet), the basis being any preferred spirit (straws optional).

GIN CRUSTA ⚱

Frost the serving glass by moistening the rim with lemon juice and then dipping in sugar; pare half a lemon and place the paring round the rim. Prepare the Crusta by filling a shaker one-third full with ice and adding 30 drops of gomme syrup (see page 25), 10 drops of Angostura, 10 drops of Curaçao and 1 wine glass London gin. Shake and strain into the serving glass.

RUM DAISY ⚱

Whereas Crustas are served cold, the ice remaining behind in the shaker, Daisies are 'on the rocks' drinks with raspberry syrup, lemon juice and fruit being added to the spirit chosen.

Fill a goblet with ice. Put in a shaker $1\frac{1}{2}$ oz rum, $\frac{3}{4}$ oz raspberry syrup and the juice of $\frac{1}{2}$ lemon. Shake and strain into the goblet. Add soda and garnish with fruit.

BRANDY FIX

Fixes are served in old fashioned glasses. Lemon, sugar, water and fruit are the usual ingredients added to the spirit selected.

Place in a tumbler 1 teaspoonful of icing sugar, $\frac{1}{2}$ wine glass water, the juice and peel of $\frac{1}{4}$ lemon and 1 wine glass brandy. Fill the tumbler two-thirds full of shaved ice, stir and garnish.

CUPS (COLD)

Not a very appropriate name for summer drinks prepared in large jugs! The basis is usually wine, with perhaps a little spirit to enliven them, some liqueurs to sweeten and cucumber, strawberries, mint and so on to be sure they look attractive.

Vyvyan Holland preferred a sparkling mosel cup. A large lump of ice (slow to melt) went into a very large jug, followed by the sparkling wine, a jigger ($1\frac{1}{2}$ oz) brandy, a pint of soda water and several dashes of a cherry liqueur. Fruit *in the jug* clouds a white wine cup, so only floating decor, such as borage and cucumber, was permitted, the cup – to preserve its sparkle – being stirred thrice only with a large spoon. (A Champagne Cup could be made similarly, but see also Fizzes, Buck's.)

Leaflets on wine cups, available free from many off-licences, are published by the Wine Development Board, Kennet Wharf Lane, London E.C.4.

SANGRIA

Since clouding red wine hardly matters, the lump of ice, the sliced apples, oranges, lemons and peaches *precede* the contents of a bottle of red wine when making this popular Spanish cup. Top up with soda last, and, ideally, keep the jug in the refrigerator for an hour before serving. A little cinnamon can be added with advantage; sugar likewise, if a sweeter version is required.

CIDER CUP

Put in the bowl 2 pints sweet cider, 1 bottle soda water, 1 wine glass sherry, $\frac{1}{2}$ wine glass brandy, the juice of $\frac{1}{2}$ lemon and the rind of a quarter of it. Flavour with sugar and nutmeg, decorate with verbena and borage. Strain and stand in the refrigerator until cold.

BEER CUP

To $1\frac{1}{2}$ oz gin, add the juice of $\frac{1}{2}$ lemon, 1 bottle lager, 1 bottle ginger beer and a splash of soda water. Garnish with a slice of cucumber and a sprig of mint; add ice and stir slightly.

FIZZES

Not unexpectedly, these are drinks that fizz. American taste is for spirit-based long drinks with a form of sweetener; in short a Sour, made to fizz with soda water or other aerated beverages. For example, a Gin Fizz comprises a measure of gin, the juice of a lemon and a teaspoonful of sugar, shaken, strained and topped with soda water. By following the suggestions I have given under Sours, all manner of fizzes can be made with whisky, sloe gin, vodka, etc. Of the recipes below (both wine fizzes) Buck's Fizz reminds me that Black Velvet – half champagne, half Guinness – is some sort of fizz too, acclaimed, at different times, by Bismarck, Gerald du Maurier and Cyril Ray.

BUCK'S FIZZ

In a big champagne glass or goblet put the juice of a fresh orange and fill with iced champagne.

MERRY WIDOW FIZZ 🍸

Shake together a large measure of Dubonnet, smaller measures of lemon and orange juice and the white of 1 egg. Strain and top up with soda water. (In the U.S.A. this fizz is made of gin and citric juices.)

FLIPS AND EGG NOGGS

A Flip is any liquor shaken with sugar and a whole egg, which is 'flipped in'. To me it looks to be an identical twin to the Egg Nogg.

The three ingredients – 1 jigger ($1\frac{1}{2}$ oz) spirits or wine, 1 teaspoonful of sugar and 1 whole egg – are shaken, strained and served with a pinch of grated nutmeg in a medium size wine glass. Among many good bases are sherry, port and 1 part Rye whiskey mixed with 1 part madeira. I particularly commend the Coffee Flip as an excellent finale for a Welsh XV's light luncheon at Twickenham; it should improve England's chances considerably.

COFFEE FLIP 🍸

15 jiggers ($22\frac{1}{2}$ oz) cognac, 15 jiggers ($22\frac{1}{2}$ oz) port, 15 eggs and a send-off of Irish Coffee liqueur. Ice well, shake and serve to every bearer of a red shirt.

RUM NOGG 🍸

Shake together 1 egg, a tot of dark rum, 1 teaspoonful of sugar and a little milk. Strain into a goblet and grate nutmeg on top.

FRAPPES

Frapper being the French verb 'to break', this term relates to drinks served with broken up or crushed ice (as opposed to cubes; i.e. 'on the rocks'). The ice goes first into a long or medium glass, followed by a liqueur and two straws. Crème de Menthe Frappé, far the best known, adds a touch of green gaiety after supper on a hot summer night. Equal parts Kummel, green Chartreuse and brandy make a stronger one; black coffee, similarly shaken with a tot of cognac, a weaker one.

HIGHBALLS

The term is American and to us their highball glass is a good sized tumbler. David Embury, seeking to simplify nomenclature, defines a Highball as any long iced drink consisting of a base liquid (alcoholic or non-alcoholic) combined with a carbonated beverage but *without citrus juices.*

Since the origin was probably a whisky and soda, the Anglo-Indian's Burra Peg and the Anglo-Malayan's Stengah are both Highballs. Others include whisky topped with cider, known as a Stonefence, gin and ginger beer and my old naval friend, the Horse's Neck – but not the John Collins because it contains lemon juice.

The Cassis Coolers, described under Wine Coolers, page 110, are also Highballs. Indeed in this entanglement of European and American names, I was fascinated to find an instance of Franco-American accord in which Canon Kir is turned into a fireman. Simon and Embury books both agree that one squirt of soda water converts a Vermouth Cassis into a Highball called Pompier.

JULEPS

Behold this cordial Julep here,
That foams and dances in his crystal bounds,
With spirits of balm and fragrant syrups mix'd.

Milton

Most of the books are wrong; the derivation is Persian, *julap* (a sweetened draught). Milton's foaming child, adopted later by Southern States parents in America, was described ecstatically by Captain Marryat (1792–1848) who had first met the mint julep in the sweltering heat of South Carolina. This was the recipe he gave:
'Put into a tumbler about a dozen sprigs of the tender shoots of mint, upon them put a spoonful of white sugar and equal proportions of brandy and peach brandy, so as to fill up one third. Then take rasped or pounded ice and fill up the tumbler. Epicures rub the lip of the tumbler with a piece of fresh pineapple, and the tumbler itself is often encrusted outside with stalactites of ice. And as this ice melts you drink.'
Had the first Bourbon distillery (1835) existed, he would have had an

even better mint julep. Although Juleps with Rye whiskey, rum, gin, brandy and apple brandy are good, the experts say that the supreme mint julep deserves the best Kentucky Bourbon. There is a possible alternative – Southern Comfort, the 100° proof Bourbon-based liqueur, flavoured with peach liqueur and fresh peaches – invented about 1875 by Louis Herron, bartender at St. Louis, Missouri.

MINT JULEP

First, frost highball glasses (or mugs with handles) for 30 minutes in the refrigerator. Place in a jug a dozen sprigs of fresh mint, 3–4 tablespoonfuls of sugar syrup and (optional) 2–3 dashes of Angostura. Gently bruise the mint and mix the three together. Add a jigger ($1\frac{1}{2}$ oz) Bourbon for each glass required and mix further. Remove glasses from refrigerator, pack with crushed ice and fill them, through a strainer, from the jug. Stir with a long spoon, adding more ice until the glasses start to frost. Garnish with sugared mint and serve with straws.

NON-ALCOHOLIC DRINKS

For the good host these are important in that guests who do not wish to drink alcohol for reasons of health, driving or personal preference, should be put at ease. With the aid of French Sirops, such as Cassis (blackberry), Framboise (raspberry), Grenadine (pomegranate), all natural fruit juices, refreshing non-alcoholic drinks of the same colour as the alcoholic drinks can be prepared as well.

APPLEADE

Slice two large apples, pour 1 pint boiling water upon them. Strain and sweeten. Serve when cold with ice.

CINDERELLA

Mix together equal parts of lemon, orange and pineapple juices.

TOMATO JUICE

Add dashes of Worcestershire sauce and celery salt to the measure required.

POUSSE CAFES

A New Orleans invention, served in a special glass, long and cylindrical like a champagne flute glass, the successful Pousse Café is a rainbow of liqueurs and a real test of a bartender's skill. The liqueurs, in order of greatest density, have to be poured into the glass so that they sit on top of one another and do not run together.

With a steady hand, some succeed in pouring down the side of the glass from a sherry glass or a spoon; others hold the spoon inside the glass, pouring over its back.

A table of densities is impracticable. Barmen follow the rule of thumb – 'the less alcoholic, the heavier the ingredient'. Thus, being heavy, non-alcoholic syrups, i.e. Grenadine or raspberry, are poured first and a strong liqueur such as green Chartreuse (96° proof) last. Experiment with any of the following, pouring in the order given:
(1) Grenadine (rose); (2) crème de cacao (brown); (3) Parfait d'amour (violet); (4) maraschino (white); (5) orange Curaçao (orange); (6) crème de menthe (green); (7) cognac (amber).

SANTINAS POUSSE CAFÉ

Pour in order: (4), (5) and (7).

AMERICAN FLAG POUSSE CAFÉ

Pour in order: (1), (3) and (4).

PARISIAN POUSSE CAFÉ

Pour in order: orange Curaçao, kirshwasser, cognac, green Chartreuse.

Three to seven differently coloured ingredients can be used, rounded off with a wallop of sweet cream on top. Finally, lest British Rail is tempted to open Pousse Café bars in Sealink ships to enliven tedious Channel crossings, I must report (with relief) that any jar or movement of the glass causes the liqueurs, running together, to make the Pousse Café look like a motorway pile-up in technicolour.

PUNCHES (COLD)

Many estates are spent in the getting,
Since women, for tea, forsook spinning and knitting
And men, for punch, forsook hewing and splitting.

17th Century Proverb

Punches, though I give them a separate heading, could really be combined with Cups. *Punj* is Sanskrit for five and the five ingredients were spirit, water, lemon, sugar and spice. The first recipes, brought back by Englishmen from the East Indies, must have been supplanted soon after by the capture of Jamaica and its rum in 1655, even though out there British seamen drank their daily tots, of no less than half a pint, neat until 1740.

In the London taverns, which in the late 17th century served as hotels and clubs, the English climate was enough to turn Punch into a hot drink – with hot water, tea, lemon, nutmeg and other spices. Each profession had its own favourite meeting place and, with the Tories drinking fine wines at Ozinda's in Pall Mall, the Whigs – the poorer party round the corner at the St. James's – took to Punch. The punchbowl, in fact, became their emblem, hung outside by enterprising taverners to attract Whigs, big and small, inside. Inn signs such as 'Crown and Punchbowl', 'Dog and Punchbowl', 'Magpie and Punchbowl' still exist.

The punchbowl became both a rallying point and, literally, the centre of conversation. Traditionally the host makes the Punch in front of his guests, which caused one old peer to say that, whereas his wine was recommended by his wine merchant, he was really proud of his Punch having made it himself.

Nevertheless – the world's hot spots outnumbering the cold – iced, not spiced, Punches still predominate and there are scores of recipes. Some, like the Duke of Norfolk's (1665), are old and need time to make and mature; others, including some which gained prizes in a London *Evening Standard* competition in recent years, require foreign fruits difficult to buy.

Each of the following should give 20 people about ½ pint each.

FISH HOUSE PUNCH

A celebrated Philadelphia Club recipe of 1732: 12 oz sugar, 3 pints water, $1\frac{1}{2}$ pints lemon juice, 2 bottles rum, 1 bottle grape brandy and $4\frac{1}{2}$ oz peach brandy.

Dissolve the sugar in a little water in the punchbowl. Add the lemon and the rest of the water, stirring well. Add the liquors, stir and allow to stand for several hours. Before serving put a big block of ice in the bowl; serve when cold.

PLANTERS' PUNCH

3 bottles white rum, 1 wine glass Grenadine, the juice of 10 limes (or lemons), Angostura, 4 pints soda water, oranges, pineapple, cherries.

Mix the rum, the Grenadine and the lime juice in the punchbowl. Shake some Angostura over the mixture. Stand in the refrigerator for 2–3 hours. Add a big block of ice, diluting with cold soda water before serving. Garnish with the fruit.

CHAMPAGNE PUNCH

4 ripe pineapples, 1 lb sugar, 1 pint lemon juice, $4\frac{1}{2}$ oz maraschino, $4\frac{1}{2}$ oz Curaçao, 1 bottle grape brandy, 1 bottle Jamaica rum, 8 bottles champagne.

Peel, slice and cube the pineapples, place in a glass bowl, cover with sugar and stand for 2–3 hours. Add the lemon juice, liqueurs, brandy and rum. Mix thoroughly and leave overnight. Before serving, transfer to a punchbowl with a large block of ice. Add the champagne when iced.

POWELL AND MOYA PUNCH

Serves $\frac{1}{2}$ pint each to 12–15 people. This will not be found in other books. Having lived for almost thirty years in a Powell and Moya house, I include this Punch as a tribute to its inventor, Sir Philip Powell. It certainly went down well with friends and fellow architects at his Silver Wedding party.

1 bottle gin, $1\frac{1}{2}$ pints French vermouth, $\frac{1}{4}$ bottle grape brandy, 2 dashes of Angostura and a little red wine to colour. Mix with ice and 3 pints fizzy lemonade (4 later when the architects have become as high as some of their buildings). Garnish with available assorted fruits.

RICKEYS

Any member of the American Bartenders' Guild will tell you that this drink came from Shoemaker's restaurant in Washington, known as 'the third house of Congress'. One hot day, circa 1900, the barman squeezed the juice of fresh limes into a gin and, after a squirt of soda water, handed it to one Colonel Jim Rickey. Since then a Rickey has evolved into any spirit-based drink, with fresh limes if you can get them, or with any other fruit if you can't. For a change I give a vodka recipe, but Rickeys of gin, sloe gin and rum are probably the best.

VODKA RICKEY

Stir in a tumbler the juice of a small lime, 1 teaspoonful of sugar (or a liqueur such as Galliano) and $1\frac{1}{2}$ oz vodka. Add ice cubes, charge glass with soda water and stir with a spoon. (Using orange juice instead of lime gives you a Harvey Wallbanger Sour.)

ROCKEFELLERS

This name, entirely my own for reasons I have already given, groups the miscellany of unnamed drinks, hard or soft, spirit-based or wine-based, served in a tall glass with a lump of ice in it. The original Rockefeller was associated with Remsen, a brand of Scotch whisky no longer in production. Indubitably the best known in the lives of British naval officers of my generation has been the Horse's Neck, the great brandy and ginger ale reviver.

HORSE'S NECK

Some recipes make it with gin or whisky. André Simon gives one with mint but no liquor. The Royal Navy puts two or three cubes of ice in a tumbler, adds a tot of grape brandy and fills up with ginger ale. Add either a slice of lemon or, more professionally, peel a large lemon in one continuous spiral. The last bit should *hang over* the outside of the glass as a reminder of what, with luck, it might cure.

MOSCOW MULE

A measure of vodka, the juice of a lemon, ice and ginger beer. Decorate with mint.

PORT AND LEMON

Make it as for a Horse's Neck, with a good measure of ruby port for the brandy and lemonade for the ginger ale.

BLACK RUSSIAN

2 parts vodka to 1 part Kahlúa, the Mexican coffee liqueur, much in vogue on both sides of the Atlantic. Serve with ice; water or soda optional.

SANGAREES

Since this drink has a bloody derivation (*sangre* is Spanish for 'blood') it ought to be red, but anything goes – from beer and stout to sherry and spirits – *provided* grated nutmeg is sprinkled on top.

PORT WINE SANGAREE

To $1\frac{1}{2}$ oz port add 1 teaspoonful of sugar. Serve in a tumbler with crushed ice, add a slice of lemon and don't forget the nutmeg and some straws.

SLINGS

Pride of place goes to Pimm's No. 1 described as the 'original gin sling'. Of the five other Pimms previously made, No. 6 (vodka-based) is now on the market again. At home, 1 part gin, 2 parts cherry brandy, the juice of a lemon, ice and soda water will make a gin sling.

I define a Sling as the British Empire name for a Rickey. Maybe they were downing them at Raffles Hotel in Singapore before that Washington colonel existed!

SINGAPORE SLING

Mix 2 parts gin with 1 part cherry brandy and 1 part lemon juice. Pour over ice in a tumbler, adding soda.
Bénédictine and brandy, a little of each, may be added just before garnishing with fresh mint and orange.

SMASHES

Mixed iced drinks flavoured with mint (see Juleps, page 102). There is also a silly Hollywood drink, the Zombie, which is a peculiar rum punch made with four rums, one of them 151° proof.

SOURS

A glance back through the list of cocktails shows that they divide fairly well into two classes; those in which the particular spirit is given an aromatic flavour with bitters or vermouth, and those in which it is given a fruit flavour with lime, lemon or orange. The fruit flavoured drinks are called Sours, the definition of a Sour being a spirit-based drink with citrus fruit juice and, usually, a sweetener. The bitters and vermouth flavoured drinks, of less use as Coolers, can be called Aromatics. Among cocktails they may outnumber the Sours, but of the basic cocktails I have already described (see The Big Seven, page 18), four – the White Lady, Daiquiri, Sidecar and Jack Rose – are Sours.

Adding more ice and some soda will convert any of these four cocktails into a long, cooling Sour. 8 parts of the chosen spirit, 2 parts lemon juice and 1 part sugar syrup are the suggested proportions for gin, rum, whiskey, brandy and applejack Sours. Other spirits may be substituted – vodka, acquavit, kirsch for example – and in place of sugar syrup the Sour could be sweetened with a liqueur, such as Cointreau, or a non-alcoholic cordial such as Grenadine.

Extending these variations to all those cocktails mainly made of a spirit and citrus juice, should keep the amateur barman as happy as the most fastidious football pool promoter engaged with his rather different permutations, but to avoid getting too mixed up with the mixing, a few points are worth remembering:

Whisky and grape brandy
a) are interchangeable;
b) do not mix as well with citrus fruits as do gin and rum;
c) are best sweetened with aromatic liqueurs like Chartreuse and Bénédictine and with orange flavours such as Curaçao and Grand Marnier, which, being of high strength, incur high duty in Britain.

Dry liquors work quicker than sweet; a strong dry Martini illustrates the point admirably. Eggs, cream and sugar, by making drinks smoother, disguise their alcoholic strength.

SYLLABUBS

These mixtures of wine, sugar and fresh cream or milk (Zabaglione for example) are desserts, best created in the kitchen, not the bar. A simple recipe is to beat together 1 part cream sherry, 1 part milk and 1 part double cream with sugar. Port or madeira are substitutes for sherry, lemon juice for milk. Serve with a spoon.

TODDIES (COLD)

Usually sweetened *hot* drinks (see page 119). Americans take a cold Toddy in which half a lump of sugar is crushed with Bourbon whiskey and ice.

WINE COOLERS

Cassis de Dijon is regarded as the best of many blackcurrant cordials, which include the British brand, Ribena. Pleasant just with iced water, an even more acceptable cooler is a glass of dry white wine, having added 1 part of the cordial to 4 parts of the wine.

The best Burgundian form is a teaspoonful of crème de cassis (the liqueur) added to Aligoté or other inexpensive white burgundy, often called a Kir, after Canon Kir, resistance hero and Mayor of Dijon. A vermouth-cassis uses dry vermouth in place of light white wine.

A Caplat – good sound Macon Blanc with Dubonnet – is popular at the Garrick Club and, so I am told by a member of both institutions, The Royal Yacht Squadron.

All these wine coolers are good summer apéritifs, but when feeling too lethargic even to mix a drink, a bottle of wine – vin blanc or vin rosé – straight or with ice in the glass, is a cooler *par excellence*.

ZOOMS

A spirit-based American drink with honey and cream. The original recipe was 8 parts cognac, 2 parts cream and 1 part honey shaken with ice.

Opposite *American Flag Pousse Café*

WARMERS

Sip your spirits and cure your cold, but I will take
Port that will cure all things, even a bad character.
For there never was a port drinker who lacked friends
to speak for him.

Thackeray

Opposite *Mulled Cider*

In spite of Thackeray's noble statement and, indeed, the Portuguese, for whom port is 'The cure for all ills save death', truth requires me to say that alcohol, far from warming the body, lowers its temperature. By dilating the blood vessels, it spreads the blood to the surfaces of the body, which loses heat more rapidly in consequence. Kept warm by other means, alcohol will stimulate the heart and cheer the imbiber. The Englishman drinking a hot whisky before going to a warm bed is sensible; the French farmer downing a neat calvados for breakfast – without food or hot coffee – before a wintery day's work in the fields, is not.

My headings, arranged alphabetically, group many individual drinks (often with curious, yet unrevealing names, such as Bang and Huckle-my-Buff) under the names of their principal ingredient.

ALE

Apples and ale combine in various forms. In Vol. III of *The Family Friend*, 1850, a Bang was a pint of cider with another of warm ale, to which sugar, grated nutmeg, ginger and a tot of whisky were added. Sugar and nutmeg also sweeten and flavour Lamb's Wool (2 pints hot ale with the pulp of 6 roasted apples) which once kept Samuel Pepys playing cards until 2 a.m. Brasenose Ale and a Jingle are similar.

BROWN BETTY

Sweetened with 4 oz brown sugar this combines 2 pints ale with ½ pint brandy. Dissolve the sugar in 1 pint water, add a slice of lemon, cloves and cinnamon. Stir well and add two slices of toast sprinkled with nutmeg and ginger. Heat.

MULLED ALE

Dissolve some sugar with boiling water in a heatproof container. Flavour with nutmeg and cinnamon. Fill almost to the top with strong ale, and heat – not necessarily with a white-hot poker – without boiling.

PURL

Gin and beer being a Dog's Nose, Purl, I fancy, qualifies as a hot Dog's Nose. It is hot ale added to a tot of gin and bitters, waiting for it in a pint tankard.

BLAZERS

These are set alight, not – as I innocently thought – named after cricketers.

For a Brandy Blazer put a lump of sugar, a twist of lemon peel, a twist of orange peel and a tot of brandy into a flameproof mug or tankard. Light the mixture, stir and strain.

A Blue Blazer is made similarly with whisky and honey.

CIDERS

Mulled cider can be useful for a party. For 12 people take 4 pints cider, 2 teaspoons brown sugar, a pinch of cloves, a little cinnamon and ginger, a wine glass of brandy or rum and slices of orange or lemon. Add the spirit *after* heating the cider, sugar and spices nearly to boiling point. Decorate with fruit and serve in heatproof mugs.

EGG DRINKS

With two jugs, 2 pints strong ale, 3–4 eggs beaten with 4 oz moist sugar, a little nutmeg and $\frac{1}{4}$ bottle rum or brandy, try your hand at an Ale Flip. Heat the ale to below boiling point and put in one jug, mixing the remaining ingredients in the other. Mix the two, tossing from one jug to the other. Huckle-my-Buff is Sussex slang for a mixture of eggs, beer and brandy.

HOT EGG NOGG

Mix equal measures of rum and brandy with 1 egg and 1 teaspoonful of sugar in a tall glass. Fill with hot milk, stir and add grated nutmeg before serving.

TOM AND JERRY

First beat the yolk and white of 1 egg separately; then beat 1 teaspoonful of sugar into the egg yolk and mix in the egg white and a tot of dark rum. Put into a mug, fill with boiling water and add a dash of brandy. Top with grated nutmeg before serving.

POSSETS

These are sweetened and spiced egg or milk drinks made with ale or white wine or sherry. The technique is to boil the wine and milk together until the milk curdles. Strain off the whey and dissolve sugar in it. Strain the curded mixture through a sieve, add spices, beat into the sweetened whey and serve hot.

If eggs are used, the yolks are beaten to a froth with the sugar and spices; the hot wine is then poured into the mixture.

GINGER WINES

Crabbies or Stone's Ginger Wine, half and half with Scotch whisky, constitutes the Whisky Mac. Brandy, gin, rum and vodka Macs are equally hot numbers according to Crabbies of Leith, who first made their Green Ginger there in 1801 when, just across the North Sea, Nelson was clapping his telescope to his blind eye at Copenhagen.

IRISH COFFEE

Nothing less than a recipe from an Irish distiller will suffice here and I quote that of A. C. Crichton of Irish Distillers Ltd. taken from *Wines and Spirits of the World*.

'Preheat the stemmed glasses in which it should be served. Over 2 lumps of sugar and a jigger of Irish pot still whiskey pour *really* hot black coffee. Stir vigorously and top with a layer of fresh cream poured gently over a spoon poised near the surface, or use slightly whipped cream. Do *not* stir or let the spoon into the glass. The charm of the drink is the hot, punch-like coffee coming through the cool cream.'

MULLS

The main merit of mulled wine is that cheap wine – even wine too old to be drinkable otherwise – is as good as any other. Consequently there are scores of recipes, all described by Raymond Postgate as elegant variations upon one primary combination like the *Kama Sutra*, which, I seem to remember, Aldous Huxley called 'Mrs. Beeton's Book of Lovemaking'.

Mulls being principally Christmas party drinks, the equipment needed is a pan holding 3–4 pints of liquid, a plastic funnel and 5–8 oz goblets unlikely to crack. The 'Compleat Muller' will have already bought sugar, lemon, grapefruit, pineapple, blackcurrant juice, canned strawberries, nutmeg, cinnamon, cloves and honey. Always heat to *below* boiling point, keeping the mull hot with a red-hot poker, or by pouring into warm bottles and standing them in a hot bath or basin. A boiled mull soon loses its 'kick'.

Mulling reminds me of my garden compost heap; certain materials are essential but more or less anything can be popped in to advantage. Wine, sugar and spices are the essentials; fruits and a glass or two of liqueurs (orange Curaçao particularly) the accessories.

The following recipes should serve about 20 people.

VIN CHAUD

2 bottles red wine, 2 large tots of brandy, 2 small cans strawberries, 4 tablespoons sugar, 2 tablespoons honey, cinnamon, 2 small cans pineapple cubes, 2 pints hot water.
Heat all ingredients except the pineapple and the hot water. Add these last and serve hot.

DR. JOHNSONS CHOICE

2 bottles red wine, 2 wine glasses orange Curaçao, 2 wine glasses brandy, 24 lumps of sugar, 12 cloves, 2 pints boiling water, grated nutmeg.
Heat wine with sugar and cloves to near boiling point. Add 2 pints of near boiling water, the orange Curaçao and the brandy. Serve with grated nutmeg.

THE BISHOP

This drink has quite a history. Dean Swift wrote of it, Dr. Johnson liked to make it and the Pickwickians drank lots of its weaker brother, the Negus, at the Rochester ball.
1½ bottles port, 2 oranges, cloves, 1 pint hot water, mixed spices and 2 oz lump sugar.
Stick one orange with cloves and roast it. Heat the port in a pan to near boiling point. Boil the water, adding spices. Add this water, the spices and the roasted orange to the hot port. Rub the lump sugar on the rind of the second orange, putting it into a bowl with half the juice of the orange. Pour the hot port mixture into the bowl. Serve as hot as possible.

NEGUS

Colonel Francis Negus was M.P. for Ipswich from 1717 to 1732, at which date Dean Swift would have been 65 and Dr. Johnson 23. Finding some political discussion between his friends becoming too acrimonious, he decided to cool their tempers while warming their bodies by diluting the port with boiling water. His recipe uses lemons instead of oranges (as in The Bishop) and dilutes $1\frac{1}{2}$ bottles of port with double that quantity of hot water.

PUNCHES (HOT)

If, as we have seen, cold Punches are much the same as cold Cups, then Mulls and hot Punches must be as closely related, except that hot Punches – as a rule laced with spirits – are the stronger brethren.

In its simplest form Punch is rum and water and I have no doubt the switch from cold to hot began when British officers and men returned home from the West Indies, dilution with hot water or hot tea being encouraged by their wives to keep them sober.

My first recipe comes from Mrs. Beeton of immortal memory; it should serve up to twenty.

HOT PUNCH BEETON

1 bottle brandy, 1 bottle dark rum, 2 lemons, 4 oz sugar, cinnamon, grated nutmeg, cloves, $2\frac{3}{4}$ pints boiling water.
Rub the rind of the lemons with the sugar. Put the sugar and remaining ingredients in a pan, heat to below boiling point and add the juice from the lemons.

RUM PUNCH

1 bottle rum, 1 bottle brandy, $\frac{1}{2}$ bottle sherry, 2 lemons, 4 oz sugar, 1 teaspoonful of ginger, up to $3\frac{1}{2}$ pints boiling water, grated nutmeg.
Grate the rind of the lemons into a small earthenware bowl and add the sugar. Macerate sugar and lemon gratings, add the juice of the lemons and the ginger. Mix well and place in another large earthenware bowl previously heated. Then add, in the following order, the rum, the brandy, the sherry and the boiling water. Mix well, sweeten further if desired, stand near heat for 20 minutes before serving in glasses or mugs, with a grating of nutmeg on top.

GLOGG

A formidable Swedish Christmas drink based on cognac.
¾ bottle sherry, 1½ bottles cognac, 4 oz sugar, 12 cloves, cinnamon,
raisins, unsalted almonds.
Omitting the sherry, put all the ingredients in a heatproof bowl.
Warm, ignite and stir until sugar is dissolved and the flame dies.
Stir in the sherry and serve while hot. (Bottle any Glogg remaining
and lightly cork; reheat to below boiling point when required.)

TODDIES (HOT)

Toddies are no more than spirits and hot water, usually sweetened,
with a slice of lemon added. Rum and whisky toddies are the most
popular, particularly for relieving a cold in the head.

STANDARD RECIPE

A measure of the spirit desired, 1 teaspoonful of sugar, 2 cloves, a
slice of lemon, a stick of cinnamon. Add boiling water in a tumbler
and stir.

GROG

A toddy made with dark rum and lemon juice; a Hot Buttered
Rum is similar, with a slice of butter instead of lemon juice.

ATHOLL BROSE

The more liquid form is really a toddy and a cold 'cure',
requiring two measures of Scotch whisky to be sweetened
with a little honey and served with hot water. The true Scot,
however, first makes his Brose steeping oatmeal with three times as
much water overnight. He then mixes in a basin: 7 parts Brose,
7 parts whisky, 5 parts cream and 1 part honey. Some porridge!

WASSAIL BOWL

Wassail, an old English greeting implying 'Good Health', gradually
became associated with mid-winter, a time when healths are drunk;
hence a bowl for the liquor in which to drink them.

Recipes for the bowl vary; the beer version is similar to Brown Betty
(see page 114) and the no beer version to The Bishop (see page 117).

EPILOGUE

Didn't we have a lovely evening?
Our party was a great success.
Didn't Mrs. Jones look stunning?
Did you notice Mrs. Brown's new dress?
What did Mr. Brown say to Uncle Benny?
Just one of those things, he'd had a few too many.
Wasn't it a hungry crowd?
They didn't leave a drop for Rover.
We ought to feel real proud.

No more anything to drink.
Leave those dishes in the sink.
What's to do about it?
Let's put out the lights and go to bed.

Rudy Vallee song of the Thirties

PARTY PIECE

Except that in the 'breath-taking' Seventies Mr. Brown had better let Mrs. Brown drive him home, parties don't change much, so here's a tip or two.

Parties need planning so have a little book in which to note, first, the number of guests you are asking. Plan enough food and drink for *all* these people and, if only about 85% come, there should be a bit left over for Rover . . . or for you? Drinks, being ready to serve, are easier than food; and, with sale or return terms, unopened bottles can be returned for cash afterwards.

Count your own glasses. If you want more, or yours are too good to risk breakage, ask your drinks supplier about his loan service; ask in good time, particularly towards December and January. The service usually is free with your order. Perhaps, if your refrigerator isn't big enough, his advice on where to find an 'ice-man' may be needed too.

Avoid complications. The pleasure of a party is diminished if hosts dash around non-stop trying to serve all manner of party foods and drinks.

'Sherry 6–8 p.m.' may still be *de rigueur* in the Cathedral Close, where archdeacons and canons residentiary can be relied upon to depart the very moment all the canapés have been gobbled. For the younger laity, sound red and white wines are probably better – and in large sizes. Not every guest, however, may want to drink wines or spirits, which is why soft drinks should always be available and displayed. Apart from children and old people, even Uncle Benny may have signed the pledge by now.

Wine and cheese buffets are popular because they are easy to run and not too expensive. 4–6 ounces of cheese and half to three-quarters of a bottle of wine is a sound estimate of consumption a head, with, of course, crisp French bread . . . and butter, funds permitting.

Port is superb with Stilton, Gorgonzola a little strong for the finest wines. Otherwise most cheeses go with most wines and there is no need to find a beautiful Brie as a companion for a handsome burgundy, or to worry about claret being suitable for Caerphilly.

To save labour, if three to five wines are put on tables, guests can help themselves. Given a bowl or two of clean water and a glass cloth, they can even rinse and retain their glasses. Nothing like making the guests do the work!

The most remarkable cocktail party I recall took place in a light cruiser, *H.M.S. Black Prince*, lying alongside in Sydney harbour, close to where the great Opera House now stands. Early in 1945, freed from the invasion of Europe, the British Pacific Fleet, an impressive force of aircraft carriers, battleships, cruisers and destroyers steamed into Sydney harbour to help end the war with Japan, and those present will never forget that Australian welcome, nor the hospitality.

To repay it, our small wardroom looked like a cross between a chemist's window and a witches' cauldron. Three huge glass containers, filled respectively with red, white and blue liquors each emitting red, white and blue smoke, lay along the mess tables. They were, in fact, all filled with White Ladies; a clever young engineer officer, after doctoring them with different colouring agents, had charged them suitably with CO_2 ice to make them smoke. Not perhaps a ploy for the parlour in the semi-detached, but nice work if you can do it.

Nowadays, in civilian life, 'cocktail parties' are more often 'wine parties'. Sparkling wines, imparting the party spirit quickly, appeal too because they have only to be poured out, not mixed. However, if the age of leisure really has arrived, there may be nothing else to do but mix cocktail ingredients all day, for parties all night, until North Sea oil and the money run out.

Since this book abounds with recipes for alcoholic drinks, my last recipes are non-alcoholic.

BUCK'S NURSERY FIZZ

Equal parts of orange juice and dry ginger ale. Serve well iced in champagne glasses with frosted rims.

HIMBEERSAFT

(*Himbeer* is raspberry in German.)
1 part raspberry syrup to 4 parts soda water.

HOME-MADE LEMONADE

Wash 3 lemons, cut each in half and squeeze the juice. Pare off the rinds, putting them in a basin with 4–6 oz castor sugar. Add $1\frac{1}{2}$ pints boiling water, cover and leave until cold, stirring occasionally. Strain into a tall 2-pint jug, add the lemon juice and chill well before serving decorated with fruit and mint.

ORANGE AND GRAPEFRUIT CUP

Mix 8 parts orange juice with 4 parts grapefruit juice, 2 parts sugar and 1 part lemon juice, stirring well. Add fresh water and ice and decorate with mint.

SHIRLEY TEMPLE

Put an ice cube and 5 dashes of Ribena or Grenadine in a champagne glass. Fill with ginger ale and decorate with fruit.

TOO MUCH OF A GOOD THING

Don't have any more, Missus Moore,
Missus Moore, please don't have any more.
The more you have the more you want, they say,
But enough is as good as a feast any day.
If you have any more, Missus Moore,
You'd never get to your street door.
Too many double gins, give the ladies double chins,
So don't have any more, Missus Moore.

Music hall song by Lily Morris

Alcohol is a good thing, but, unfortunately, a poison. Drunk men tell no lies and an extremely drunk man in a Maltese bar once told me that alcohol always caught you up; perhaps the same night, possibly the next morning, or it might wait slyly for years to give you a stroke or cirrhosis at sixty.

So far, it has always given me a headache the next morning. Once I consulted a Harley Street Ear, Nose and Throat surgeon saying that I felt the headache's severity was out of all proportion to the alcohol consumed. He was sympathetic. After explaining what a high pressure flow of pink gin was doing to my sinus, he said, 'It's a pity, but I am sure you would not like my operation; you're much better off with your hangover.'

Being a sympathiser, I will give some 'corpse revivers' even though I doubt their efficacy. Protein protection for the stomach lining before the debauche, afforded by meat, eggs or milk does more good. If – before the Old Reprobates' annual orgy for example – a 'protein high tea' is hardly practicable, try 2 ounces of olive oil instead. Avoid sweet drinks, sugar is an ally of the demon alcohol.

Sad to relate, abuse of alcohol – a cause of road deaths and much human unhappiness through alcoholism – has increased to a point where an Alcohol Education Centre (with which the Wine and Spirit Trade collaborates) has been established. The Government is expected to issue health warnings. Maximum employment and education for leisure would help in the long term, meanwhile moderation remains an unsatisfactory, yet vital, counsel.

🍸 = Shaker 🥛 = Mixing Glass

CORPSE REVIVER 1 🍸

Shake together 1 part brandy, 1 part Fernet-Branca and 1 part white crème de menthe.

CORPSE REVIVER 2 🍸

Shake together 1 oz brandy, 4 oz milk, a dash of Angostura and 1 teaspoonful of sugar. Serve in a tumbler with soda.

PRAIRIE OYSTER

Pour into a wine glass 1 teaspoonful of Worcestershire sauce, 1 teaspoonful of tomato juice, the yolk of 1 raw egg, and 2 dashes of vinegar, taking care not to break the egg yolk. Add a dash of pepper.

BULL SHOT 🍸

Vigorously shake together 1 oz vodka, 2 oz condensed consommé, 2 oz tomato juice and a dash of Worcestershire sauce, Tabasco, cayenne and celery salt.

PICK-ME-UP COCKTAIL 🥛

Mix 1 part cognac with 1 part dry vermouth and 1 part Pastis.

INDEX

ΒΥ ΤΗΕ SΑΜΕ ΑUTHΟR

Wine Mine, A First Anthology (Ed.), 1970.
Guide to Visiting Vineyards, 1977.
Off the Shelf, Gilbey Vintners' Guide to Wines and Spirits, 1972 and 1977.